THE SELECTED POEMS OF
SIR CHARLES G. D. ROBERTS

THE SELECTED POEMS OF
SIR CHARLES G. D. ROBERTS

Edited with an Introduction by
DESMOND PACEY

McGRAW-HILL RYERSON LIMITED

Toronto   Montreal

PREFACE

IT IS now seventy-five years since Charles Roberts' first book of poems heralded the dawn of a new era in Canadian literature, and twenty years since his own selected edition of his poetry appeared. It should be possible, then, to see his work in perspective and to begin the process of deciding what parts of it are worthy of permanent remembrance. This book is offered as a contribution to these ends.

I wish to thank those who have helped me in the selection of these poems—Dr. Lorne Pierce of The Ryerson Press, and Dr. Alfred G. Bailey and Dr. Fred Cogswell of the University of New Brunswick. Part of the research required for the introduction was made possible by a grant in aid from the Humanities Research Council of Canada, to whose members I am most grateful.

DESMOND PACEY

University of New Brunswick,
Fredericton, N.B.
April 1, 1955.

TABLE OF CONTENTS

INTRODUCTION

SIR CHARLES G. D. ROBERTS has a secure place in the literary history of Canada. He was the acknowledged leader of our first significant poetic movement, the movement which, in the eighties and nineties of the last century, brought the people and especially the landscape of the young nation to the attention of the English-speaking world. In those two decades, Roberts himself, his cousin Bliss Carman, Archibald Lampman, Duncan Campbell Scott, William Wilfred Campbell, George Frederick Cameron, and Pauline Johnson were publishing regularly in the leading magazines of Canada, the United States and Great Britain. And the books these writers produced were being enthusiastically reviewed in the same magazines. Never before, and unfortunately never since, has Canadian writing attracted so much attention both at home and abroad.

If Roberts had done nothing but stimulate this movement, he would deserve our remembrance and gratitude. And stimulate it he did. It was he who encouraged his younger cousin Bliss Carman to devote himself to a literary career; the publication of his *Orion and Other Poems* in 1880 opened the eyes of Archibald Lampman and other budding poets to the fact that poetry could indeed be written and published in Canada; during his editorship of *The Week* magazine he found space to publish the early poems of Lampman and Carman; he contributed literary criticism of a high standard to *The Week* and other Canadian and American magazines; he carried on an active correspondence with most of the young Canadian writers of his time and was always ready to give them encouragement and constructive criticism.

But his role was not restricted to that of a catalyst. He wrote copiously himself, and proved himself adept in a great variety of literary forms. In addition to his poetry, he wrote the animal stories which became perhaps the most popular type of short story on the North American continent about the turn of the century, a history of Canada which was the first to unite a respect for the facts with a concern for literary style, and novels which combined accurate description of the Canadian landscape with a romantic re-creation of the Canadian past.

Poetry, however, was his first and his last love. He wrote his stories and novels at least in part to please the public and to make money; he wrote his poems to express his real convictions and insights and to satisfy his own creative urge. As time passes, it becomes clear that it is primarily as a poet that Roberts will be remembered. That is as he would have wished it to be.

.   .   .

His poetic career was, in relation to his lengthy life, a short one. Almost all his best poetry was produced in two periods, the first extending from roughly 1885 to 1895, the second from 1925 to 1935. There was a rapid development, a sudden decline, a long silence, and a late revival. How may this unusual pattern be explained?

The reasons for Roberts' rapid development are not far to seek. He was born, on January 10, 1860, of a family both sides of which for generations had taken a keen interest in literary and scholarly matters. His birthplace, Douglas near Fredericton, is one of the most beautiful spots on the bank of the stately Saint John River. His early boyhood was spent at Westcock, in the Tantramar region of New Brunswick—a region which, by its unusual beauty of waving marsh grasses, surging tidal streams and rivers, and red tide flats, is likely to inspire a poetic response even in the most insensitive persons. At the age of fourteen he returned to Fredericton, where he was able to attend the Collegiate School and the University of New Brunswick at a time when those institutions were enjoying a period of intense intellectual activity. At the Collegiate School he came under the influence of George Parkin, recently returned from Oxford and filled with high enthusiasm for the poetry of Rossetti and Swinburne. At the university he had as stimulants the energetic and cultured president, Brydone Jack, the versatile Thomas Harrison, himself later president of the college, the dynamic George E. Foster, later to become, next to Laurier, the greatest orator in Canadian public life, and such fellow-students as John Douglas Hazen, Bliss Carman, H. V. B. Bridges, and W. S. Carter, all of whom later had distinguished careers.

But it was not only the immediate environment of Fredericton that was a source of stimulation to the young poet in his formative years. He grew up in the eighteen-seventies, when the current of national idealism which had issued in Confederation was still running strongly. Canadian intellectuals and public men such as G. Mercer Adam, Charles Mair, Edward Blake, and the Canada First party were declaring that the young nation needed a literature to give it a sense of cohesion and common purpose. Magazine and newspaper articles were clamouring for poets and novelists to put into permanent literary form the aspirations of the Canadian people and the distinctive features of the Canadian land.

Thus the young Roberts had every encouragement to try his wings as a poet, and when *Orion and Other Poems* appeared in 1880 it was greeted with a chorus of approval. It gave him such standing that within three years, when he was still only twenty-three, he was offered and accepted the editorship of *The Week*, founded by Goldwin Smith as the chief intellectual and literary magazine of its time. When he resigned from *The Week*, because his views favouring Canadian Independence clashed with Smith's Annexation-ist sympathies, he had little difficulty in securing a pro-fessorship at King's College, Windsor, Nova Scotia.

King's College was an almost ideal situation for a young writer. It had a lovely natural setting, a small but eager group of professors and students, and an administration which recognized the value of Roberts' literary work and made his academic duties as light as possible so that he could devote much of his time to writing. During the long summer vacations he had abundant leisure, and the stimulating companionship of visiting writers such as Richard Hovey and Bliss Carman. The result was that in the ten years of his professoriate, from 1885 to 1895, he did his best work as a poet and laid the foundations of his later reputation as a writer of short stories and novels. His services as a public lecturer were in demand in such centres as Quebec, Montreal, New York and Boston; and his literary and scholarly standing was such that in 1890, at the early age of thirty, he was elected a Fellow of The Royal Society of Canada.

And yet, in spite of all these advantages, this apparent plethora of opportunities in his own land, Roberts resigned his professorship in 1895, two years later left Canada for the United States, and to all intents and purposes put poetry behind him for almost thirty years. Why?

In part, of course, the reason is to be found in the poet's own character. He frankly admits, in several of his poems, that he was always temperamentally restless, that he found it hard to stay in one place or at one task for very long. James Cappon, by far the most acute critic of Roberts' poetry, has pointed to the lack of a moral centre in the verse, and we may assume that this is attributable to a certain moral instability in the man. The King's College post was honourable, useful, convenient—but it was not very exciting, and it must at times have seemed almost too easy, not quite worthy of the poet's many talents. Moreover, the salary was pitifully small—only a thousand dollars a year—and the poet had a wife and several children to support. There must have been a great temptation to believe that the salary was not worth the restrictions the position imposed on him. And there was family trouble too, trouble the precise nature of which it is too early to more than guess at—but we do know that when Roberts left Canada, he left his wife and family behind him. Although he wrote to his wife and occasionally sent her money, he never lived with her again for any prolonged period. Whatever other reasons we may adduce, we must be willing to recognize that these personal factors may alone have been decisive.

But there were other factors which must have had some effect. There was first of all his reception by the critics, a reception which was, to put it mildly, injudicious. From first almost to last, Canadian critics over-praised Roberts, and on the rare occasions when they attacked him they nearly always attacked him for the wrong reasons. In particular, they encouraged him to believe that his talents were wasted on the simple description of his Maritime environment, and that he should essay the role of the philosophical and prophetic poet. Most of them ignored the fact that Roberts had found his true métier in the straightforward objective poems of *Songs of the Common Day* (1893), and praised him for turning, in *The Book of the Native* (1896), to what they called loftier themes. The insidious suggestion that anything would be better than to describe the scenes and people among whom he had grown up was continually being made, and in view of its frequency our wonder grows not that Roberts left the Maritimes so soon but that he dared to stay so long.

The critics, then, must certainly bear their share of the blame for Roberts' decline as a poet. On the one hand, they encouraged him to believe that his early poetry was so faultless that there was no challenge to improve it; on the other, they encouraged him to attempt a kind of poetry to which he was not suited.

Another factor was the decay of Canadian idealism. The first two decades following Confederation were disappointing from a material standpoint—the transcontinental railway took much longer to complete than had been foreseen, for much of the time there was an economic depression—but they were full of intellectual promise and achievement. Various forms of federation, reorganization and expansion brought new life to the universities; the Royal Society of Canada was founded to foster scholarly activity in the arts, letters, and sciences; magazines, newspapers, and books of surprisingly high calibre were published; Canadian painting began to develop under the stimulus of the Royal Canadian Academy and the Toronto Art Students' League; debates in the new Canadian parliament were conducted at a relatively high level of oratorical style and political thought. And then, in the mid-nineties, this first national intellectual movement began to falter. The Royal Society, founded with so much enthusiasm, began to have difficulty in attracting a quorum of Fellows to its annual meeting; the best of the magazines, *The Week*, ceased publication in 1896; more and more of the brightest young Canadians began to emigrate to the United States. Writers especially began to leave the country. Most of them—Roberts, Carman, Peter McArthur, Arthur Stringer, Norman Duncan, E. W. Thomson—went to the United States; a few—Robert Barr, Gilbert Parker—went to Great Britain. Just as, with the accession of Laurier to power in 1896, economic expansion set in at a rapid pace, intellectual development began to slow down. For the next quarter century, Canadians (with, of course a few exceptions, notably the painters of the Group of Seven) seemed almost to forget the idealistic spirit in which Confederation had been born and to place all their emphasis on material wealth.

Roberts himself was far from immune to the new materialism. He had grown up during the idealistic first two decades of Canadian nationality, and had been inspired by his spiritual environment to write his poems of direct and indirect patriotism. But the tangible results had been meagre, and the most substantial cheques had come not from Canadian but from American sources, and not for poetry but for prose. When he first visited New York in the

eighties he had heard the siren call of American dollars, and
had written the humorous verses, "The Poet Is Bidden to
Manhattan Island":

> Dear Poet, quit your shady lanes
> And come where more than lanes are shady.
> Leave Phyllis to the rustic swains
> And sing some Knickerbocker lady.
> O hither haste, and here devise
> Divine *ballades* before unuttered.
> Your poet's eyes *must* recognize
> The side on which your bread is buttered.
>
> .   .   .
>
> You've piped at home, where none could pay,
> Till now, I trust, your wits are riper,
> Make no delay but come this way,
> And pipe for them that pay the piper.

But Roberts' nationalism was sufficiently strong that he was
able to resist this seductive invitation for another ten years.
As late as May, 1895, *The Week*, presumably on Roberts'
own authority, was able to assure its readers that the poet
would not leave his native country:

> Some recent paragraphs have appeared in the provincial
> press to the effect that Mr. C. G. D. Roberts had resigned
> the chair of English in King's College and would hereafter
> devote himself entirely to literature and reside in the States.
> The first of these statements is unfortunately true. . . .
> One part of the report, however, is fortunately not true.
> Professor Roberts does not propose to leave Canada and
> take up his residence in the United States. Owing to the
> lack of a literary career in Canada, it is necessary that one's
> literary work should be marketed in the States, but Roberts
> is too thorough a Canadian to leave his own country
> permanently. His tastes and sympathies are all Canadian,
> and however lofty a place he may win in the literary world
> Canada will be able to claim him as her son.

There is no reason to doubt that Roberts was sincere in his
resolution at this time; but after a year and a half of free-
lancing from Fredericton, he was offered and accepted the

post of assistant editor of *The Illustrated American*, and left for New York in February, 1897. He did not return permanently to Canada until February, 1925.

Self-exile need not have brought a prolonged halt in Roberts' progress as a poet, but in fact it did. Had he dedicated himself to the gradual fashioning of his memories of his native country into artistic form, he might have become the truly great national poet his ardent admirers claimed him to be. Instead, he was bewitched by the goddess of Success. It was much more exciting to be a literary celebrity abroad than to be a smalltown professor at home. He dined and wined in the company of lords and ladies, even breakfasted on one occasion with the King. He was forever on the move: from New York he went on, in 1907, to Paris, thence to Munich, and then to London, which served as his headquarters from 1912 to 1925. He had a full and exciting life, he gave distinguished service during the First World War, he even wrote a quantity of reputable prose, but poetry he almost entirely neglected. As far as his poetry is concerned, these years from 1897 to 1925 are the lost years.

It must have been something of a surprise to Roberts to find, on his return to Canada in 1925, that he was still venerated as the great national poet. A new burst of national idealism and intellectual awakening had followed World War I, and Roberts was acclaimed as one of its heroes. Under the stimulus of such adoration—it is scarcely too strong a word for the enthusiasm which everywhere greeted him—he turned again to his old love, and produced two or three small books containing poems which had something of his old mastery. Once more he was universally regarded as the leading man of letters in the Dominion, and when a literary man was to be selected for a knighthood, in 1935, the choice of Roberts for the honour was regarded as inevitable and proper.

But it was too late to expect a really new departure in his poetic art. Although he declared in the preface to his

Selected Poems that "from early youth to the present day I have always been alive to the moment, keenly aware of contemporary currents of thought, action and emotion," he was really out of touch with the new literary ideals in Canada. He seemed to the experimental young poets of the twenties and thirties to have nothing to say to them, to be in fact the living symbol of a tradition which they rejected.

What we must seek to do now is to rescue Roberts' reputation from his too fervent admirers on the one hand and his too bitter detractors on the other. As we have seen, there are ample reasons to account for his desertion of Canada and poetry. We must now be ready to give him credit for what he did achieve in the brief span of his poetic creativity, to examine that work impartially in the effort to discover its real strengths and weaknesses. For although the man died on November 26, 1943, the poems live on.

.   .   .

The poems for which Roberts is likely to be remembered were produced, as we have seen, in two periods of creative activity, one extending from the early eighteen-eighties to the early eighteen-nineties, and the other from the mid-nineteen-twenties to the mid-nineteen-thirties. There are minor differences in the poems of the two periods—the early ones are in traditional metres, and especially in the form of sonnets and elegies, the later ones are in free verse—but their characteristics are basically the same. The best poems from both periods fall into three main classes: objective descriptive poems in which Roberts reveals his talent as a painter in words; lyrics in which he expresses his own moods of elation, restlessness, nostalgia, or despair; and more pretentious poems in which he seeks by means of symbols to convey his sense of the immensity, grandeur, and power of the cosmos.

Orion and Other Poems (1880) is a good book for a young poet of twenty, but it contains none of Roberts' best work.

xix

It is the product of a mind steeped in the legends of ancient Greece and the poems of Keats, Shelley, and Tennyson. Most of its poems are artificial and derivative in language and feeling, although a few of them give evidence of genuine descriptive powers. The verse is always competent— smooth in rhythm, rich and suggestive in language, bold in imagery—but it is never very distinctive. It is the work of an apprentice, who is quite frankly serving under a sequence of masters from whom he hopes to learn his art.

In Divers Tones (1886) is still the work of an apprentice, but of an apprentice who has gone a long way toward independent mastery. There are more classical narratives in the style of Tennyson, and one of them, "Actaeon," has some magnificently sonorous lines. One new note is provided by the patriotic poems, "Collect for Dominion Day" and "Canada." These poems, and especially the latter, are apt to seem much more conventional in thought to us than they did to contemporary readers. "Canada" is a quite explicit plea for Canadian independence, made at a time when the dispute between the advocates of Independence, Imperial Federation and American Annexation was the chief political issue in the country. As such, it has at least historical interest, though it must be admitted that, like most explicitly patriotic poems, it has its share of rhetoric.

But the really remarkable development evident in this book is not that Roberts has discovered Canadian nationalism nor that he has improved his technique in the classical narrative, but that he has begun to recognize the poetic potential of his own environment. "Tantramar Revisited," and sonnets such as "The Sower" and "The Potato Harvest," are on a far higher level than anything Roberts had previously written. "Tantramar Revisited" is, if not a great, certainly a very good poem. The verse form is perfectly suited to the theme of nostalgic remembrance, and it is handled with masterly ease. And the poem has a definite and satisfying structure: we begin with ten lines in which

the poet describes his own emotional situation; then follows
the long middle section descriptive of the Tantramar region;
and the poem concludes with ten lines which bring us back
to the poet. The visual details in the middle section are
remarkable for their accuracy and for the way in which
they are woven into a pattern. And the words throughout
are chosen with a full recognition of their meaning, sugges-
tion, melody, and rhythm. There are none here of the
discordant words which so often, even in Roberts' better
poems, jar and mar the effect.

A few of the poems in *In Divers Tones*, then, are of high
quality; but they are so outnumbered by weak or derivative
ones that no one could have foreseen that Roberts' next
volume, *Songs of the Common Day* (1893) would mark such a
great advance in his art. The best parts of the new book
are the first section, which contains thirty-seven sonnets
describing various phases of Maritime life, and the last,
which takes the form of a long pastoral elegy for Shelley.
Many of the sonnets are spoiled by Roberts' two chief
faults as a poet: his tendency to lapse into a too overt and
consciously applied didacticism, and his fondness for exotic
but vague epithets. But there are a round dozen sonnets in
which these flaws are scarcely apparent and which reveal
Roberts' main strengths: the clarity and pattern of his
pictures, the exactness of his visual details, the sincerity of
his feelings, and the firm discipline of his music. We see the
landscape clearly, we infer the importance of the scene to
humanity, and we are impressed by the cunning fusion of
fact and feeling into a poetic whole.

The miscellaneous section of *Songs of the Common Day* is
less rewarding. "Marsyas" is a belated example of
Roberts' ability to handle classical legends skilfully, and
"Grey Rocks and Greyer Sea" is a pleasing short elegy with
rather too obvious Tennysonian echoes. The rest of the
section is negligible, and one or two of the poems are
ludicrous,

"Ave," however, almost attains the level of the best sonnets in the first section. Professor James Cappon put his finger on its chief weakness when he declared that the transition from the description of the Tantramar country to the account of Shelley's life is awkward and forced. Apart from this, the poem is a very satisfying exercise in the pastoral elegy. The descriptive part of the poem is surpassed only by "Tantramar Revisited," and Roberts succeeds remarkably well in recapturing the rather elusive qualities of Shelley's personality and art.

The best poems in *The Book of the Native* are those which continue the manner and matter of the sonnets in *Songs of the Common Day*. Poems such as "Where the Cattle Come to Drink," "Epitaph for a Husbandman," and "The Brook in February" have the accuracy of detail and rightness of tone which made the previous volume so impressive. But the book makes clear that Roberts had begun to move away from such poems in the direction of more pretentious poems of a philosophical and mystical turn. Some of the mystical poems are good as expressions of emotion, but their thought is hazy. Roberts can evoke a feeling of mystery and wonder, but when he goes on to philosophize he takes refuge in verbal evasions and comforting compromises. Encouraged by the critics to over-rate himself, he was obviously seeking to rise above the status of a good but limited regional poet to that of a universal prophet. He did not have the necessary qualities of mind to succeed in the attempt, and he made it at the cost of authenticity, concreteness, and distinctiveness.

If there is a slight decline in *The Book of the Native*, there is a positive descent in *New York Nocturnes* (1898). The poet himself seems conscious of weariness and a lack of true inspiration now that he has left his native Maritimes and become a New York journalist: many of the poems strike the note of ennui and frustration. The best poems in the book—"The Solitary Woodsman" and "Beyond the Tops of Time"—return to the themes of *Songs of the Common Day* and *The Book of the Native* respectively. But the general trend is away from rural vignettes and mystical contemplations to poems of love and loneliness. And these love poems have none of Roberts' clarity or discipline: they are contrived and artificial, the products of fancy rather than imagination. The impression here, contrary to that of *Songs of the Common Day*, is of an art without substance, of an inspiration which has become attenuated, of a mind which has turned in upon itself without the moral strength to make a real "confession of the ill."

In 1901 Roberts brought out his *Collected Poems*, but no new work appeared in book form until 1903, when *The Book of the Rose* was published. This is no better and no worse than its immediate predecessor: again the bulk of the contents are perfervid and artificial love poems, and the few outstanding poems—"The First Ploughing," "Child of the Infinite," and "The Great and Little Weavers"—are reversions to earlier themes. Only in two poems are there interesting new departures: "The Stranded Ship" is a vigorous ballad with a Kiplingesque swing to it, and "Heat in the City" is a vivid picture of urban suffering and squalor.

Apparently recognizing that his poetic inspiration had flagged, Roberts virtually abandoned the craft for the next twenty-five years. A revised edition of his *Collected Poems* appeared in 1907, a slim volume of *New Poems* in 1919, and a Ryerson Poetry Chapbook, *The Sweet o' the Year*, in 1925, but these contained little that was new and still less that was of lasting interest. *New Poems*, in spite of the fact that it was the product of a sixteen year period, contains only twenty-five poems, of which but three or four have any real distinction. *The Sweet o' the Year*, apart from the doggerel-like title poem, consists wholly of reprintings from *New Poems*.

It was *The Vagrant of Time* (1927) that marked the beginning of the late revival of Roberts' poetic art. The book contains only about a dozen new poems, but they are almost all good and they reveal a genuine development in Roberts' poetic technique. There is evident a greater freedom of verse form, a readiness to experiment with new metres, greater simplicity and naturalness of diction. Some of the poems, and notably "Philander's Song," have the frank, relaxed, gay manner which makes Yeats' last phase so delightful. Others—the title poem, "In the Night Watches," "Hath Hope Kept Vigil"—are more serious in theme and manner, but no less liquid and pleasing.

The revival was continued in *The Iceberg and Other Poems* (1934). In addition to the splendid title poem, this book contains "Taormina," a haunting, vivid, nostalgic poem bright with colour and subtle in music, "Be Quiet, Wind," a lyric replete with sweet sadness, and "Westcock Hill," a poem nostalgic of his childhood home which communicates real emotion by means of precise but suggestive images. But "The Iceberg" is the pride of the book. A long narrative poem in free verse, it reveals how economically and functionally Roberts had learned to use this treacherous form. Some of the descriptive passages are magnificent, and the whole poem has life and movement on the one hand and a firm orderly structure on the other. Many of the metaphors and similes are very striking, and the ending has a magic that reminds us of the closing lines of "Actaeon."

Roberts' last book of poems, *Canada Speaks of Britain* (1941), was published early in the Second World War as a patriotic offering. Its contents added little to his reputation, but one of the poems, "Two Rivers," is interesting biographically. Clear-sighted about his own character, Roberts sees his own restlessness reflected in the constant ebb and flow of the tide-driven Tantramar:

> Across the estranging, changing years,
>   Blind puppet of my restless star,
> In discontent content alone,
>   You urge and drive me, Tantramar.

xxiv

Restlessness—this is the clue to Roberts' career. It drove him from Fredericton to Toronto to Windsor; for a few years he seemed to have conquered it and settled down to produce his best work; then it drove him forth again—to New York, London, and the Continent—until, for the last eighteen years of his life, he found a haven again in his native Canada. But his restlessness was not a mere itch to travel. It led him to try his hand at almost every literary form except drama, to become a kind of literary jack-of-all-trades. Above all, for our present purposes, it led him to give up the kind of poetry for which he was especially gifted to write the philosophical verse the critics urged upon him and the exotic lyrics that were popular in the magazines. And it led him to leave even the poems of his own special sort marred by imperfections of diction which some steady and determined revision might quickly have removed. No doubt he had a full, active, and happy life—but he left us only a slim volume of good poems. However, a life that produced the poems in this book was far from being lived in vain, and Sir Charles G. D. Roberts' most fitting monument is before you.

ORION AND OTHER POEMS
1880

SIR CHARLES G. D. ROBERTS

Portrait by John Russell, 1934

From ORION

       . . . SUDDEN the day
Brake full.   The healing of its radiance fell
Upon his eyes, and straight his sightless eyes
Were opened.   All the morning's majesty
And mystery of loveliness lay bare
Before him; all the limitless blue sea
Brightening with laughter many a league around,
Wind-wrinkled, keel-uncloven, far below;
And far above the bright sky-neighbouring peaks;
And all around the broken precipices,
Cleft-rooted pines swung over falling foam,
And silver vapours flushed with the wide flood
Of crimson slanted from the opening east
Well ranked, the vanguard of the day,—all these
Invited him, but these he heeded not.
For there beside him, veiléd in a mist
Where—through the enfolded splendour issued forth,—
As delicate music unto one asleep
Through mist of dreams flows softly,—all her hair
A mist of gold flung down about her feet,
Her dewy, cool, pink fingers parting it
Till glowing lips, and half-seen snowy curves
Like Parian stone, unnerved him, waited SHE,—
Than Circe skilfuller to put away
His pain, to set his sorrow afar off,—
Eos, with warm heart warm for *him*.   His toils
Endured in vain, his great deeds wrought in vain,
His bitter pain, Œnopion's house accurst,
And even his sweet revenge, he recked not of;
But gave his heart up straightway unto love.

IN DIVERS TONES

1886

CANADA

O CHILD of Nations, giant-limbed,
  Who stand'st among the nations now
Unheeded, unadored, unhymned,
  With unanointed brow,—

How long the ignoble sloth, how long
  The trust in greatness not thine own?
Surely the lion's brood is strong
  To front the world alone!

How long the indolence, ere thou dare
  Achieve thy destiny, seize thy fame—
Ere our proud eyes behold thee bear
  A nation's franchise, nation's name?

The Saxon force, the Celtic fire,
  These are thy manhood's heritage!
Why rest with babes and slaves?   Seek higher
  The place of race and age.

I see to every wind unfurled
  The flag that bears the Maple Wreath;
Thy swift keels furrow round the world
  Its blood-red folds beneath;

Thy swift keels cleave the furthest seas;
  Thy white sails swell with alien gales;
To stream on each remotest breeze
  The black smoke of thy pipes exhales.

O Falterer, let thy past convince
  Thy future,—all the growth, the gain,
The fame since Cartier knew thee, since
  Thy shores beheld Champlain!

Montcalm and Wolfe! Wolfe and Montcalm!
    Quebec, thy storied citadel
Attest in burning song and psalm
    How here thy heroes fell!

O Thou that bor'st the battle's brunt
    At Queenston, and at Lundy's Lane,—
On whose scant ranks but iron front
    The battle broke in vain!—

Whose was the danger, whose the day,
    From whose triumphant throats the cheers,
At Chrysler's Farm, at Chateauguay,
    Storming like clarion-bursts our ears?

On soft Pacific slopes,—beside
    Strange floods that northward rave and fall,—
Where chafes Acadia's chainless tide—
    Thy sons await thy call.

They wait; but some in exile, some
    With strangers housed, in stranger lands,—
And some Canadian lips are dumb
    Beneath Egyptian sands.

O mystic Nile! Thy secret yields
    Before us; thy most ancient dreams
Are mixed with far Canadian fields
    And murmur of Canadian streams.

But thou, my Country, dream not thou!
    Wake, and behold how night is done,—
How on thy breast, and o'er thy brow,
    Bursts the uprising sun!

From ACTÆON

I HAVE lived long, and watched out many days,
Yet have not seen that aught is sweet save life,
Nor learned that life hath other end than death.
Thick horror like a cloud had veiled my sight,
That for a space I saw not, and my ears
Were shut from hearing; but when sense grew clear
Once more, I only saw the vacant pool
Unrippled,—only saw the dreadful sward,
Where dogs lay gorged, or moved in fretful search,
Questing uneasily; and some far up
The slope, and some at the low water's edge,
With snouts set high in air and straining throats
Uttered keen howls that smote the echoing hills.
They missed their master's form, nor understood
Where was the voice they loved, the hand that reared;—
And some lay watching by the spear and bow
Flung down.

      And now upon the homeless pack
And paling stream arose a noiseless wind
Out of the yellow west awhile, and stirred
The branches down the valley; then blew off
To eastward toward the long grey straits, and died
Into the dark, beyond the utmost verge.

THE TANTRAMAR REVISITED

SUMMERS and summers have come, and gone with the
    flight of the swallow;
Sunshine and thunder have been, storm, and winter, and
    frost;
Many and many a sorrow has all but died from remem-
    brance,
Many a dream of joy fall'n in the shadow of pain.

Hands of chance and change have marred, or moulded, or
    broken,
Busy with spirit or flesh, all I most have adored;
Even the bosom of Earth is strewn with heavier shadows,—
Only in these green hills, aslant to the sea, no change!
Here where the road that has climbed from the inland
    valleys and woodlands,
Dips from the hill-tops down, straight to the base of the
    hills,—
Here, from my vantage-ground, I can see the scattering
    houses,
Stained with time, set warm in orchards, meadows, and
    wheat,
Dotting the broad bright slopes outspread to southward
    and eastward,
Wind-swept all day long, blown by the south-east wind.

Skirting the sunbright uplands stretches a riband of
    meadow,
Shorn of the labouring grass, bulwarked well from the sea,
Fenced on its seaward border with long clay dikes from the
    turbid
Surge and flow of the tides vexing the Westmoreland
    shores.
Yonder, toward the left, lie broad the Westmoreland
    marshes,—
Miles on miles they extend, level, and grassy, and dim,
Clear from the long red sweep of flats to the sky in the
    distance,
Save for the outlying heights, green-rampired Cumberland
    Point;
Miles on miles outrolled, and the river-channels divide
    them,—
Miles on miles of green, barred by the hurtling gusts.

Miles on miles beyond the tawny bay is Minudie.
There are the low blue hills; villages gleam at their feet.
Nearer a white sail shines across the water, and nearer
Still are the slim, grey masts of fishing boats dry on the
     flats.
Ah, how well I remember those wide red flats, above tide-
     mark
Pale with scurf of the salt, seamed and baked in the sun!
Well I remember the piles of blocks and ropes, and the net-
     reels
Wound with the beaded nets, dripping and dark from the
     sea!
Now at this season the nets are unwound; they hang from
     the rafters
Over the fresh-stowed hay in upland barns, and the wind
Blows all day through the chinks, with the streaks of sun-
     light, and sways them
Softly at will; or they lie heaped in the gloom of a loft.

Now at this season the reels are empty and idle; I see them
Over the lines of the dikes, over the gossiping grass.
Now at this season they swing in the long strong wind,
     thro' the lonesome
Golden afternoon, shunned by the foraging gulls.
Near about sunset the crane will journey homeward above
     them;
Round them, under the moon, all the calm night long,
Winnowing soft grey wings of marsh-owls wander and
     wander,
Now to the broad, lit marsh, now to the dusk of the dike.
Soon, thro' their dew-wet frames, in the live keen freshness
     of morning,
Out of the teeth of the dawn blows back the awakening
     wind.

Then, as the blue day mounts, and the low-shot shafts of the
    sunlight
Glance from the tide to the shore, gossamers jewelled with
    dew
Sparkle and wave, where late sea-spoiling fathoms of drift-
    net
Myriad-meshed, uploomed sombrely over the land.

Well I remember it all.   The salt raw scent of the margin;
While, with men at the windlass, groaned each reel, and the
    net,
Surging in ponderous lengths, uprose and coiled in its
    station;
Then each man to his home,—well I remember it all!

Yet, as I sit and watch, this present peace of the land-
    scape,—
Stranded boats, these reels empty and idle, the hush,
One grey hawk slow-wheeling above yon cluster of hay-
    stacks,—
More than the old-time stir this stillness welcomes me home.
Ah the old-time stir, how once it stung me with rapture,—
Old-time sweetness, the winds freighted with honey and
    salt!
Yet will I stay my steps and not go down to the marsh-
    land,—
Muse and recall far off, rather remember than see,—
Lest on too close sight I miss the darling illusion,
Spy at their task even here the hands of chance and change.

THE SOWER

A BROWN, sad-coloured hillside, where the soil,
    Fresh from the frequent harrow, deep and fine,
    Lies bare; no break in the remote sky-line,
Save where a flock of pigeons streams aloft,
Startled from feed in some low-lying croft,
    Of far-off spires with yellow of sunset shine;
    And here the Sower, unwittingly divine,
Exerts the silent forethought of his toil.

Alone he treads the glebe, his measured stride
    Dumb in the yielding soil; and though small joy
    Dwell in his heavy face, as spreads the blind
Pale grain from his dispensing palm aside,
    This plodding churl grows great in his employ;—
    Godlike, he makes provision for mankind.

THE POTATO HARVEST

A HIGH bare field, brown from the plough, and borne
    Aslant from sunset; amber wastes of sky
    Washing the ridge; a clamour of crows that fly
In from the wide flats where the spent tides mourn
To yon their rocking roosts in pines wind-torn;
    A line of grey snake-fence, that zigzags by
    A pond and cattle; from the homestead nigh
The long deep summonings of the supper horn.

Black on the ridge, against that lonely flush,
    A cart, and stoop-necked oxen; ranged beside,
    Some barrels; and the day-worn harvest-folk,
Here, emptying their baskets, jar the hush
    With hollow thunders. Down the dusk hillside
    Lumbers the wain; and day fades out like smoke.

SONGS OF THE COMMON DAY
1893

THE COW PASTURE

I SEE the harsh, wind-ridden, eastward hill,
   By the red cattle pastured, blanched with dew;
   The small, mossed hillocks where the clay gets through;
The grey webs woven on milkweed tops at will.
The sparse, pale grasses flicker, and are still.
   The empty flats yearn seaward. All the view
   Is naked to the horizon's utmost blue;
And the bleak spaces stir me with strange thrill.

Not in perfection dwells the subtler power
   To pierce our mean content, but rather works
   Through incompletion, and the need that irks,—
Not in the flower, but effort toward the flower.
   When the want stirs, when the soul's cravings urge,
   The strong earth strengthens, and the clean heavens
      purge.

WHEN MILKING TIME IS DONE

WHEN milking time is done, and over all
   This quiet Canadian inland forest home
   And wide rough pasture-lots the shadows come,
And dews, with peace and twilight voices, fall,
From moss-cooled watering-trough to foddered stall
   The tired plough-horses turn,—the barnyard loam
   Soft to their feet,—and in the sky's pale dome
Like resonant chords the swooping night-jars call.

The frogs, cool-fluting ministers of dream,
   Make shrill the slow brook's borders; pasture bars
   Down clatter, and the cattle wander through,—
Vague shapes amid the thickets; gleam by gleam
   Above the wet grey wilds emerge the stars,
   And through the dusk the farmstead fades from view,

THE SALT FLATS

HERE clove the keels of centuries ago
   Where now unvisited the flats lie bare.
   Here seethed the sweep of journeying waters, where
No more the tumbling floods of Fundy flow,
And only in the samphire pipes creep slow
   The salty currents of the sap.   The air
   Hums desolately with wings that seaward fare,
Over the lonely reaches beating low.

The wastes of hard and meagre weeds are thronged
With murmurs of a past that time has wronged;
   And ghosts of many an ancient memory
Dwell by the brackish pools and ditches blind,
In these low-lying pastures of the wind,
   These marshes pale and meadows by the sea.

THE PEA-FIELDS

THESE are the fields of light, and laughing air,
   And yellow butterflies, and foraging bees,
   And whitish, wayward blossoms winged as these,
And pale green tangles like a seamaid's hair.
Pale, pale the blue, but pure beyond compare,
   And pale the sparkle of the far-off seas,
   A-shimmer like these fluttering slopes of peas,
And pale the open landscape everywhere.

From fence to fence a perfumed breath exhales
   O'er the bright pallor of the well-loved fields,—
My fields of Tantramar in summer-time;
   And, scorning the poor feed their pasture yields,
Up from the bushy lots the cattle climb,
   To gaze with longing through the grey, mossed rails.

THE MOWING

THIS is the voice of high midsummer's heat.
  The rasping vibrant clamour soars and shrills
  O'er all the meadowy range of shadeless hills,
As if a host of giant cicadae beat
The cymbals of their wings with tireless feet,
  Or brazen grasshoppers with triumphing note
  From the long swath proclaimed the fate that smote
The clover and timothy-tops and meadowsweet.

The crying knives glide on; the green swath lies.
  And all noon long the sun, with chemic ray,
  Seals up each cordial essence in its cell,
That in the dusky stalls, some winter's day,
  The spirit of June, here prisoned by his spell,
  May cheer the herds with pasture memories.

THE OAT-THRESHING

A LITTLE brown old homestead, bowered in trees
  That o'er the autumn landscape shine afar,
  Burning with amber and with cinnabar.
A yellow hillside washed in airy seas
Of azure, where the swallow drops and flees.
  Midway the slope, clear in the beaming day,
  A barn by many seasons beaten grey,
Big with the gain of prospering husbandries.

In billows round the wide red welcoming doors
  High piles the golden straw; while from within,
  Where plods the team amid the chaffy din,
The loud pulsation of the thresher soars,
  Persistent as if earth could not let cease
  This happy proclamation of her peace.

THE WINTER FIELDS

WINDS here, and sleet, and frost that bites like steel.
  The low bleak hill rounds under the low sky.
  Naked of flock and fold the fallows lie,
Thin streaked with meagre drift.   The gusts reveal
By fits the dim grey snakes of fence, that steal
  Through the white dusk.   The hill-foot poplars sigh,
  While storm and death with winter trample by,
And the iron fields ring sharp, and blind lights reel.

Yet in the lonely ridges, wrenched with pain,
  Harsh solitary hillocks, bound and dumb,
Grave glebes close-lipped beneath the scourge and chain,
  Lurks hid the germ of ecstasy—the sum
Of life that waits on summer, till the rain
  Whisper in April and the crocus come.

IN AN OLD BARN

TONS upon tons the brown-green fragrant hay
  O'erbrims the mows beyond the time-warped eaves,
  Up to the rafters where the spider weaves,
Though few flies wander his secluded way.
Through a high chink one lonely golden ray,
  Wherein the dust is dancing, slants unstirred.
  In the dry hush some rustlings light are heard,
Of winter-hidden mice at furtive play.

Far down, the cattle in their shadowed stalls,
  Nose-deep in clover fodder's meadowy scent,
  Forget the snows that whelm their pasture streams,
The frost that bites the world beyond their walls.
  Warm housed, they dream of summer, well content
  In day-long contemplation of their dreams.

THE FLIGHT OF THE GEESE

I HEAR the low wind wash the softening snow,
   The low tide loiter down the shore.   The night
   Full filled with April forecast, hath no light.
The salt wave on the sedge-flat pulses slow.
Through the hid furrows lisp in murmurous flow
   The thaw's shy ministers; and hark!   The height
   Of heaven grows weird and loud with unseen flight
Of strong hosts prophesying as they go!

High through the drenched and hollow night their wings
   Beat northward hard on winter's trail.   The sound
Of their confused and solemn voices, borne
Athwart the dark to their long Arctic morn,
   Comes with a sanction and an awe profound,
A boding of unknown, foreshadowed things.

IN THE WIDE AWE AND WISDOM OF THE NIGHT

IN THE wide awe and wisdom of the night
   I saw the round world rolling on its way,
Beyond significance of depth or height,
   Beyond the interchange of dark and day.
I marked the march to which is set no pause,
   And that stupendous orbit, round whose rim
The great sphere sweeps, obedient unto laws
   That utter the eternal thought of Him.

I compassed time, outstripped the starry speed,
   And in my still soul apprehended space,
Till, weighing laws which these but blindly heed,
   At last I came before Him face to face,—
And knew the Universe of no such span
As the august infinitude of Man.

THE HERRING WEIR

BACK to the green deeps of the outer bay
  The red and amber currents glide and cringe,
  Diminishing behind a luminous fringe
Of cream-white surf and wandering wraiths of spray.
Stealthily, in the old reluctant way,
  The red flats are uncovered, mile on mile,
  To glitter in the sun a golden while.
Far down the flats, a phantom sharply grey,
The herring weir emerges, quick with spoil.
  Slowly the tide forsakes it.   Then draws near,
Descending from the farm-house on the height,
A cart, with gaping tubs.   The oxen toil
  Sombrely o'er the level to the weir,
  And drag a long black trail across the light.

MARSYAS

A LITTLE grey hill-glade, close-turfed, withdrawn
Beyond resort or heed of trafficking feet,
Ringed round with slim trunks of the mountain ash.
Through the slim trunks and scarlet bunches flash—
Beneath the clear chill glitterings of the dawn—
Far off, the crests, where down the rosy shore
The Pontic surges beat.
The plains lie dim below.   The thin airs wash
The circuit of the autumn-coloured hills,
And this high glade, whereon
The satyr pipes, who soon shall pipe no more.
He sits against the beech-tree's mighty bole,—
He leans, and with persuasive breathing fills
The happy shadows of the slant-set lawn.
The goat-feet fold beneath a gnarlèd root;
And sweet, and sweet the note that steals and thrills
From slender stops of that shy flute.

Then to the goat-feet comes the wide-eyed fawn
Hearkening; the rabbits fringe the glade, and lay
Their long ears to the sound;
In the pale boughs the partridge gather round,
And quaint hern from the sea-green river reeds;
The wild ram halts upon a rocky horn
O'erhanging; and, unmindful of his prey,
The leopard steals with narrowed lids to lay
His spotted length along the ground.
The thin airs wash, the thin clouds wander by,
And those hushed listeners move not.   All the morn
He pipes, soft-swaying, and with half-shut eye,
In rapt content of utterance,—
      nor heeds
The young God standing in his branchy place,
The languor on his lips, and in his face,
Divinely inaccessible, the scorn.

GREY ROCKS AND GREYER SEA

GREY rocks, and greyer sea,
 And surf along the shore—
And in my heart a name
 My lips shall speak no more.

The high and lonely hills
 Endure the darkening year—
And in my heart endure
 A memory and a tear.

Across the tide a sail
 That tosses, and is gone—
And in my heart the kiss
 That longing dreams upon.

Grey rocks, and greyer sea,
 And surf along the shore—
And in my heart the face
 That I shall see no more.

AVE!

(An Ode for the Centenary of Shelley's Birth)

I

O TRANQUIL meadows, grassy Tantramar,
  Wide marshes ever washed in clearest air,
Whether beneath the sole and spectral star
  The dear severity of dawn you wear,
Or whether in the joy of ample day
  And speechless ecstasy of growing June
You lie and dream the long blue hours away
    Till nightfall comes too soon,
Or whether, naked to the unstarred night,
You strike with wondering awe my inward sight,—

II

You know how I have loved you, how my dreams
  Go forth to you with longing, through the years
That turn not back like your returning streams
  And fain would mist the memory with tears,
Though the inexorable years deny
  My feet the fellowship of your deep grass,
O'er which, as o'er another, tenderer sky,
    Cloud phantoms drift and pass,—
You know my confident love, since first, a child,
Amid your wastes of green I wandered wild.

III

Inconstant, eager, curious, I roamed;
  And ever your long reaches lured me on;
And ever o'er my feet your grasses foamed,
  And in my eyes your far horizons shone.
But sometimes would you (as a stillness fell
  And on my pulse you laid a soothing palm),
Instruct my ears in your most secret spell;
    And sometimes in the calm
Initiate my young and wondering eyes
Until my spirit grew more still and wise.

IV

Purged with high thoughts and infinite desire
  I entered fearless the most holy place,
Received between my lips the secret fire,
  The breath of inspiration on my face.
But not for long these rare illumined hours,
  The deep surprise and rapture not for long.
Again I saw the common, kindly flowers,
    Again I heard the song
Of the glad bobolink, whose lyric throat
Pealed like a tangle of small bells afloat.

V

The pounce of mottled marsh-hawk on his prey;
  The flicker of sand-pipers in from sea
In gusty flocks that puffed and fled; the play
  Of field-mice in the vetches,—these to me
Were memorable events. But most availed
  Your strange unquiet waters to engage
My kindred heart's companionship; nor failed
    To grant this heritage,—
That in my veins forever must abide
The urge and fluctuation of the tide.

VI

The mystic river whence you take your name,
  River of hubbub, raucous Tantramar,
Untamable and changeable as flame,
  It called me and compelled me from afar,
Shaping my soul with its impetuous stress.
  When in its gaping channel deep withdrawn
Its waves ran crying of the wilderness
    And winds and stars and dawn,
How I companioned them in speed sublime,
Led out a vagrant on the hills of Time!

25

VII

And when the orange flood came roaring in
  From Fundy's tumbling troughs and tide-worn caves,
While red Minudie's flats were drowned with din
  And rough Chignecto's front oppugned the waves,
How blithely with the refluent foam I raced
  Inland along the radiant chasm, exploring
The green solemnity with boisterous haste;
    My pulse of joy outpouring
To visit all the creeks that twist and shine
From Beauséjour to utmost Tormentine.

VIII

And after, when the tide was full, and stilled
  A little while the seething and the hiss,
And every tributary channel filled
  To the brim with rosy streams that swelled to kiss
The grass-roots all awash and goose-tongue wild
  And salt-sap rosemary,—then how well content
I was to rest me like a breathless child
    With play-time rapture spent,—
To lapse and loiter till the change should come
And the great floods turn seaward, roaring home.

IX

And now, O tranquil marshes, in your vast
  Serenity of vision and of dream,
Where through by every intricate vein have passed
  With joy impetuous and pain supreme
The sharp fierce tides that chafe the shores of earth
  In endless and controlless ebb and flow,
Strangely akin you seem to him whose birth
    One hundred years ago
With fiery succour to the ranks of song
Defied the ancient gates of wrath and wrong.

X

Like yours, O marshes, his compassionate breast,
  Wherein abode all dreams of love and peace,
Was tortured with perpetual unrest.
  Now loud with flood, now languid with release,
Now poignant with the lonely ebb, the strife
  Of tides from the salt sea of human pain
That hiss along the perilous coasts of life
    Beat in his eager brain;
But all about the tumult of his heart
Stretched the great calm of his celestial art.

XI

Therefore with no far flight, from Tantramar
  And my still world of ecstasy, to thee,
Shelley, to thee I turn, the avatar
  Of Song, Love, Dream, Desire and Liberty;
To thee I turn with reverent hands of prayer
  And lips that fain would ease my heart of praise,
Whom chief of all whose brows prophetic wear
    The pure and sacred bays
I worship, and have worshipped since the hour
When first I felt thy bright and chainless power.

XII

About thy sheltered cradle, in the green
  Untroubled groves of Sussex, brooded forms
That to the mother's eye remained unseen,—
  Terrors and ardours, passionate hopes, and storms
Of fierce retributive fury, such as jarred
  Ancient and sceptred creeds, and cast down kings,
And oft the holy cause of Freedom marred
    With lust of meaner things,
With guiltless blood, and many a frenzied crime
Dared in the face of unforgetful Time.

27

XIII

The star that burns on revolution smote
   Wild heats and change on thine ascendant sphere,
Whose influence thereafter seemed to float
   Through many a strange eclipse of wrath and fear,
Dimming awhile the radiance of thy love.
   But still supreme in thy nativity,
All dark, invidious aspects far above,
      Beamed one clear orb for thee,—
The star whose ministrations just and strong
Controlled the tireless flight of Dante's song.

XIV

With how august contrition, and what tears
   Of penitential unavailing shame,
Thy venerable foster-mother hears
   The sons of song impeach her ancient name,
Because in one rash hour of anger blind
   She thrust thee forth in exile, and thy feet
Too soon to earth's wild outer ways consigned,—
      Far from her well-loved seat,
Far from her studious halls and storied towers
And weedy Isis winging through his flowers.

XV

And thou, thenceforth the breathless child of change,
   Thine own Alastor, on an endless quest
Of unimagined loveliness, didst range,
   Urged ever by the soul's divine unrest.
Of that high quest and that unrest divine
   Thy first immortal music thou didst make,
Inwrought with fairy Alp, and Reuss, and Rhine,
      And phantom seas that break
In soundless foam along the shores of Time,
Prisoned in thine imperishable rhyme,

28

XVI

Thyself the lark melodious in mid-heaven;
  Thyself the Protean shape of chainless cloud,
Pregnant with elemental fire, and driven
  Through deeps of quivering light, and darkness loud
With tempest, yet beneficent as prayer;
  Thyself the wild west wind, relentless strewing
The withered leaves of custom on the air,
    And through the wreck pursuing
O'er lovelier Arnos, more imperial Romes,
Thy radiant visions to their viewless homes.

XVII

And when thy mightiest creation thou
  Wert fain to body forth,—the dauntless form,
The all-enduring, all-forgiving brow
  Of the great Titan, flinchless in the storm
Of pangs unspeakable and nameless hates,
  Yet rent by all the wrongs and woes of men,
And triumphing in his pain, that so their fates
    Might be assuaged,—oh then
Out of that vast compassionate heart of thine
Thou wert constrained to shape the dream benign.

XVIII

—O Baths of Caracalla, arches clad
  In such transcendent rhapsodies of green
That one might guess the sprites of spring were glad
  For your majestic ruin, yours the scene,
The illuminating air of sense and thought;
  And yours the enchanted light, O skies of Rome,
Where the giant vision into form was wrought;
    Beneath your blazing dome
The intensest song our language ever knew
Beat up exhaustless to the blinding blue!—

XIX

The domes of Pisa and her towers superb,
    The myrtles and the ilexes that sigh
O'er San Giuliano, where no jars disturb
    The lonely aziola's evening cry,
The Serchio's sun-kissed waters,—these conspired
    With Plato's theme occult, with Dante's calm
Rapture of mystic love, and so inspired
        Thy soul's espousal psalm,
A strain of such elect and pure intent
It breathes of a diviner element.

XX

Thou on whose lips the word of Love became
    A rapt evangel to assuage all wrong,
Not Love alone, but the austerer name
    Of Death engaged the splendours of thy song.
The luminous grief, the spacious consolation
    Of thy supreme lament, that mourned for him
Too early haled to that still habitation
        Beneath the grass-roots dim,—
Where his faint limbs and pain-o'erwearied heart
Of all earth's loveliness became a part,

XXI

But where, thou sayest, himself would not abide,—
    Thy solemn incommunicable joy
Announcing Adonais has not died,
    Attesting death to free but not destroy,
All this was as thy swan-song mystical.
    Even while the note serene was on thy tongue
Thin grew the veil of the Invisible,
        The white sword nearer swung,—
And in the sudden wisdom of thy rest
Thou knewest all thou hadst but dimly guessed.

XXII

Lament, Lerici, mourn for the world's loss!
  Mourn that pure light of song extinct at noon!
Ye waves of Spezzia that shine and toss
  Repent that sacred flame you quenched too soon!
Mourn, Mediterranean waters, mourn
  In affluent purple down your golden shore!
Such strains as his, whose voice you stilled in scorn,
    Our ears may greet no more,
Unless at last to that far sphere we climb
Where he completes the wonder of his rhyme!

XXIII

How like a cloud she fled, thy fateful bark,
  From eyes that watched to hearts that waited, till
Up from the ocean roared the tempest dark—
  And the wild heart love waited for was still!
Hither and thither in the slow, soft tide,
  Rolled seaward, shoreward, sands and wandering shells
And shifting weeds thy fellows, thou didst hide
    Remote from all farewells,
Nor felt the sun, nor heard the fleeting rain,
Nor heeded Casa Magni's quenchless pain.

XXIV

Thou heededst not?   Nay, for it was not thou,
  That blind, mute clay relinquished by the waves
Reluctantly at last, and slumbering now
  In one of kind earth's most compassionate graves!
Not thou, not thou,—for thou wert in the light
  Of the Unspeakable, where time is not.
Thou sawest those tears; but in thy perfect sight
    And thy eternal thought
Were they not even now all wiped away
In the reunion of the infinite day!

XXV

There face to face thou sawest the living God
  And worshippedst, beholding Him the same
Adored on earth as Love, the same whose rod
  Thou hadst endured as Life, whose secret name
Thou now didst learn, the healing name of Death.
  In that unroutable profound of peace,
Beyond experience of pulse and breath,
    Beyond the last release
Of longing, rose to greet thee all the lords
Of Thought, with consummation in their words.

XXVI

He of the seven cities claimed, whose eyes,
  Though blind, saw gods and heroes, and the fall
Of Ilium, and many alien skies,
  And Circe's Isle; and he whom mortals call
The Thunderous, who sang the Titan bound
  As thou the Titan victor; the benign
Spirit of Plato; Job; and Judah's crowned
    Singer and seer divine;
Omar; the Tuscan; Milton vast and strong;
And Shakespeare, captain of the host of Song.

XXVII

Back from the underworld of whelming change
  To the wide-glittering beach thy body came;
And thou didst contemplate with wonder strange
  And curious regard thy kindred flame,
Fed sweet with frankincense and wine and salt,
  With fierce purgation search thee, soon resolving
Thee to the elements of the airy vault
    And the far spheres revolving,
The common waters, the familiar woods,
And the great hills' inviolate solitudes.

XXVIII

Thy close companions there officiated
    With solemn mourning and with mindful tears,—
The pained, imperious wanderer unmated
    Who voiced the wrath of those rebellious years;
Trelawney, lion-limbed and high of heart;
    And he, that gentlest sage and friend most true,
Whom Adonais loved.   With these bore part
        One grieving ghost, that flew
Hither and thither through the smoke unstirred
In wailing semblance of a wild white bird.

XXIX

O heart of fire, that fire might not consume,
    Forever glad the world because of thee;
Because of thee forever eyes illume
    A more enchanted earth, a lovelier sea!
O poignant voice of the desire of life,
    Piercing our lethargy, because thy call
Aroused our spirits to a nobler strife
        Where base and sordid fall,
Forever past the conflict and the pain
More clearly beams the goal we shall attain!

XXX

And now once more, O marshes, back to you
    From whatsoever wanderings near or far,
To you I turn with joy forever new,
    To you, O sovereign vasts of Tantramar!
Your tides are at the full.   Your wizard flood,
    With every tribute stream and brimming creek,
Ponders, possessor of the utmost good,
        With no more left to seek,—
But the hour wanes and passes; and once more
Resounds the ebb with destiny in its roar.

XXXI

So might some lord of men, whom force and fate
  And his great heart's unvanquishable power
Have thrust with storm to his supreme estate,
  Ascend by night his solitary tower
High o'er the city's lights and cries uplift.
  Silent he ponders the scrolled heaven to read
And the keen star's conflicting message sift,
    Till the slow signs recede,
And ominously scarlet dawns afar
The day he leads his legions forth to war.

EPITAPH FOR A SAILOR BURIED ASHORE

HE WHO but yesterday would roam
  Careless as clouds and currents range,
In homeless wandering most at home,
  Inhabiter of change;

Who wooed the west to win the east,
  And named the stars of North and South,
And felt the zest of Freedom's feast
  Familiar in his mouth;

Who found a faith in stranger-speech,
  And fellowship in foreign hands,
And had within his eager reach
  The relish of all lands—

How circumscribed a plot of earth
  Keeps now his restless footsteps still,
Whose wish was wide as ocean's girth,
  Whose will the water's will!

THE BOOK OF THE NATIVE
1896

ORIGINS

OUT OF the dreams that heap
The hollow hand of sleep,—
Out of the dark sublime,
From the averted Face
Beyond the bournes of space,
Into the sudden sun
We journey, one by one.
Out of the hidden shade
Wherein desire is made,—
Out of the pregnant stir
Where death and life confer,—
The dark and mystic heat
Where soul and matter meet,—
The enigmatic Will,—
We start, and then are still.

Inexorably decreed
By the ancestral deed,
The puppets of our sires,
We work out blind desires,
And for our sons ordain,
The blessing or the bane.
In ignorance we stand
With fate on either hand,
And question stars and earth
Of life, and death, and birth.
With wonder in our eyes
We scan the kindred skies,
While through the common grass
Our atoms mix and pass.
We feel the sap go free
When spring comes to the tree;
And in our blood is stirred
What warms the brooding bird.

The vital fire we breathe
That bud and blade bequeath,
And strength of native clay
In our full veins hath sway.

But in the urge intense
And fellowship of sense,
Suddenly comes a word
In other ages heard.
On a great wind our souls
Are borne to unknown goals,
And past the bournes of space
To the unaverted Face.

THE FROSTED PANE

ONE NIGHT came Winter noiselessly, and leaned
  Against my window-pane.
In the deep stillness of his heart convened
  The ghosts of all his slain.

Leaves, and ephemera, and stars of earth,
  And fugitives of grass,—
White spirits loosed from bonds of mortal birth,
  He drew them on the glass.

AFOOT

COMES the lure of green things growing,
Comes the call of waters flowing,—
  And the wayfarer Desire
Moves and wakes and would be going.

Hark the migrant hosts of June
Marching nearer noon by noon!
  Hark the gossip of the grasses
Bivouacked beneath the moon!

. . .

Hark the sharp, insistent cry
Where the hawk patrols the sky!
  Hark the flapping, as of banners,
Where the heron triumphs by!

. . .

Long the quest and far the ending
Where my warfarer is wending,—
  When Desire is once afoot,
Doom behind and dream attending!

Shuttle-cock of indecision,
Sport of chance's blind derision,
  Yet he may not fail nor tire
Till his eyes shall win the Vision.

In his ears the phantom chime
Of incommunicable rhyme,
  He shall chase the fleeting camp-fires
Of the Bedouins of Time.

. . .

Till, through laughter and through tears,
Fair the final peace appears,
  And about the watered pastures
Sink to sleep the nomad years!

WHERE THE CATTLE COME TO DRINK

AT EVENING, where the cattle come to drink,
  Cool are the long marsh-grasses, dewy cool
  The alder thickets, and the shallow pool,
And the brown clay about the trodden brink.
The pensive afterthoughts of sundown sink
  Over the patient acres given to peace;
  The homely cries and farmstead noises cease,
And the worn day relaxes, link by link.
A lesson that the open heart may read
  Breathes in this mild benignity of air,
  These dear, familiar savours of the soil,—
A lesson of the calm and humble creed,
  The simple dignity of common toil,
  And the plain wisdom of unspoken prayer.

AN EPITAPH FOR A HUSBANDMAN

HE WHO would start and rise
  Before the crowing cocks—
No more he lifts his eyes,
  Whoever knocks.

He who before the stars
  Would call the cattle home,—
They wait about the bars
  For him to come.

Him at whose hearty calls
  The farmstead woke again
The horses in their stalls
  Expect in vain.

Busy, and blithe, and bold,
  He laboured for the morrow,—
The plough his hands would hold
  Rusts in the furrow.

His fields he had to leave,
    His orchards cool and dim;
The clods he used to cleave
    Now cover him.

But the green, growing things
    Lean kindly to his sleep,—
White roots and wandering strings,
    Closer they creep.

Because he loved them long
    And with them bore his part,
Tenderly now they throng
    About his heart.

THE UNSLEEPING

I SOOTHE to unimagined sleep
The sunless bases of the deep.
And then I stir the aching tide
That gropes in its reluctant side.

I heave aloft the smoking hill;
To silent peace its throes I still.
But ever at its heart of fire
I lurk, an unassuaged desire.

I wrap me in the sightless germ
An instant or an endless term;
And still its atoms are my care,
Dispersed in ashes or in air.

I hush the comets one by one
To sleep for ages in the sun;
The sun resumes before my face
His circuit of the shores of space.

The mount, the star, the germ, the deep,
They all shall wake, they all shall sleep.
Time, like a flurry of wild rain,
Shall drift across the darkened pane.

Space, in the dim predestined hour,
Shall crumble like a ruined tower.
I only, with unfaltering eye,
Shall watch the dreams of God go by.

RECESSIONAL

NOW ALONG the solemn heights
Fade the Autumn's altar-lights;
   Down the great earth's glimmering chancel
Glide the days and nights.

Little kindred of the grass,
Like a shadow in a glass
   Falls the dark and falls the stillness;
We must rise and pass.

We must rise and follow, wending
Where the nights and days have ending,—
   Pass in order pale and slow
Unto sleep extending.

Little brothers of the clod,
Soul of fire and seed of sod,
   We must fare into the silence
At the knees of God.

Little comrades of the sky
Wing to wing we wander by,
   Going, going, going, going,
Softly as a sigh.

Hark, the moving shapes confer,
Globe of dew and gossamer,
  Fading and ephemeral spirits
In the dusk astir.

Moth and blossom, blade and bee,
Worlds must go as well as we,
  In the long procession joining
Mount, and star, and sea.

Toward the shadowy brink we climb
Where the round year rolls sublime,
  Rolls, and drops, and falls forever
In the vast of time;

Like a plummet plunging deep
Past the utmost reach of sleep,
  Till remembrance has no longer
Care to laugh or weep.

THE STILLNESS OF THE FROST

OUT OF the frost-white wood comes winnowing through
  No wing; no homely call or cry is heard.
  Even the hope of life seems far deferred.
  The hard hills ache beneath their spectral hue.
A dove-grey cloud, tender as tears or dew,
  From one long hearth exhaling, hangs unstirred,
  Like the poised ghost of some unnamed great bird
  In the ineffable pallor of the blue.

Such, I must think, even at the dawn of Time,
  Was thy white hush, O world, when thou lay'st cold,
  Unwaked to love, new from the Maker's word,
And the spheres, watching, stilled their high accord,
  To marvel at perfection in thy mould,
  The grace of thine austerity sublime!

THE BROOK IN FEBRUARY

A SNOWY path for squirrel and fox,
  It winds between the wintry firs.
Snow-muffled are its iron rocks,
  And o'er its stillness nothing stirs.

But low, bend low a listening ear!
  Beneath the mask of moveless white
A babbling whisper you shall hear
  Of birds and blossoms, leaves and light.

BESIDE THE WINTER SEA

AS ONE who sleeps, and hears across his dream
The cry of battles ended long ago,
Inland I hear the calling of the sea.
I hear its hollow voices, though between
My wind-worn dwelling and thy wave-worn strand
How many miles, how many mountains are!
And thou beside the winter sea alone
Art walking, with thy cloak about thy face.
Bleak, bleak the tide, and evening coming on;
And grey the pale, pale light that wans thy face.
Solemnly breaks the long wave at thy feet;
And sullenly in patches clings the snow
Upon the low, red rocks worn round with years.
I see thine eyes, I see their grave desire,
Unsatisfied and lonely as the sea's;—
Yet how unlike the wintry sea's despair!
For could my feet but follow thine, my hands
But reach for thy warm hands beneath thy cloak,
What summer joy would lighten in thy face,
What sunshine warm thine eyes, and thy sad mouth
Break to a dewy rose and laugh on mine!

AN AUGUST WOOD ROAD

WHEN THE partridge coveys fly
In the birch-tops cool and high;

When the dry cicadas twang
Where the purpling fir-cones hang;

When the bunch-berries emboss—
Scarlet beads—the roadside moss:

Brown with shadows, bright with sun,
All day long till day is done

Sleeps in murmuring solitude
The worn old road that threads the wood.

In its deep cup—grassy, cool—
Sleeps the little roadside pool;

Sleeps the butterfly on the weed,
Sleeps the drifted thistle-seed.

Like a great and blazing gem,
Basks the beetle on the stem.

Up and down the shining rays
Dancing midges weave their maze.

High among the moveless boughs,
Drunk with day, the night-hawks drowse.

Far up, unfathomably blue,
August's heaven vibrates through.

The old road leads to all things good;
The year's at full, and time's at flood.

THE WITCHES' FLIGHT

COME, Red Mouse,
  And come, Black Cat!
Oh, see what the goat
  And the toad are at!
Oh, see them where
They rise in the air,
And wheel and dance
  With the whirling bat!

We rise, we rise
  On the smoking air;
And the withered breast
  Grows young and fair;
And the eyes grow bright
With alluring light,
And the fierce mouth softens
  With love's soft prayer.

Come, White Sisters,
  Naked of limb!
The horned moon reddens;
  The stars grow dim;
The crags in the gloom
Of our caldron's fume
Shudder and topple
  And reel and swim.

We mount, we mount
  Till the moon seems nigh.
Our rout possesses
  The middle sky.
With strange embraces,
And maddened faces,
And streaming tresses,
  We twist and fly.

Come, White Sisters,
    And four-foot kin,
For the horned moon sinks
    And the reek grows thin,
And brief is the night
Of our delight,
And brief the span
    Of our secret sin.

EARTH'S COMPLINES

BEFORE the feet of the dew
There came a call I knew,
    Luring me into the garden
Where the tall white lilies grew.

I stood in the dusk between
The companies of green,
    O'er whose aerial ranks
The lilies rose serene.

And the breathing air was stirred
By an unremembered word,
    Soft, incommunicable—
And wings not of a bird.

I heard the spent blooms sighing,
The expectant buds replying;
    I felt the life of the leaves,
Ephemeral, yet undying.

The spirits of earth were there,
Thronging the shadowed air,
    Serving among the lilies,
In an ecstasy of prayer.

Their speech I could not tell;
But the sap in each green cell,
    And the pure initiate petals,
They knew that language well.

I felt the soul of the trees—
Of the white, eternal seas—
    Of the flickering bats and night-moths
And my own soul kin to these.

And a spell came out of space
From the light of its starry place,
    And I saw in the deep of my heart
The image of God's face.

TWILIGHT ON SIXTH AVENUE

OVER the tops of the houses
    Twilight and sunset meet.
The green, diaphanous dusk
    Sinks to the eager street.

Astray in the tangle of roofs
    Wanders a wind of June.
The dial shines in the clock-tower
    Like the face of a strange-scrawled moon.

The narrowing lines of the houses
    Palely begin to gleam,
And the hurrying crowds fade softly
    Like an army in a dream.

Above the vanishing faces
    A phantom train flares on
With a voice that shakes the shadows,—
    Diminishes, and is gone.

And I walk with the journeying throng
    In such a solitude
As where a lonely ocean
    Washes a lonely wood.

NEW YORK NOCTURNES

1898

NIGHT IN A DOWN-TOWN STREET

NOT in the eyed, expectant gloom,
  Where soaring peaks repose
And incommunicable space
  Companions with the snows;

Not in the glimmering dusk that crawls
  Upon the clouded sea,
Where bourneless wave on bourneless wave
  Complains continually;

Not in the palpable dark of woods
  Where groping hands clutch fear,
Does Night her deeps of solitude
  Reveal unveiled as here.

The street is a grim cañon carved
  In the eternal stone,
That knows no more the rushing stream
  It anciently has known.

The emptying tide of life has drained
  The iron channel dry.
Strange winds from the forgotten day
  Draw down, and dream, and sigh.

The narrow heaven, the desolate moon
  Made wan with endless years,
Seem less immeasurably remote
  Than laughter, love, or tears.

BEYOND THE TOPS OF TIME

HOW LONG it was I did not know,
  That I had waited, watched, and feared.
It seemed a thousand years ago
  The last pale lights had disappeared.
I knew the place was a narrow room
Up, up beyond the reach of doom.

Then came a light more red than flame;—
  No sun-dawn, but the soul laid bare
Of earth and sky and sea became
  A presence burning everywhere;
And I was glad my narrow room
Was high above the reach of doom.

Windows there were in either wall,
  Deep cleft, and set with radiant glass,
Wherethrough I watched the mountains fall,
  The ages wither up and pass.
I knew their doom could never climb
My tower beyond the tops of Time.

A sea of faces then I saw,
  Of men who had been, men long dead.
Figured with dreams of joy and awe
  The heavens unrolled in lambent red;
While far below the faces cried—
"Give us the dream for which we died!"

Ever the woven shapes rolled by
  Above the faces hungering.
With quiet and incurious eye
  I noted many a wondrous thing,—
Seas of clear glass, and singing streams,
In that high pageantry of dreams;

Cities of sard and chrysoprase
   Where choired Hosannas never cease;
Valhallas of celestial frays,
   And lotus-pools of endless peace;
But still the faces gaped and cried—
"Give us the dream for which we died!"

At length my quiet heart was stirred,
   Hearing them cry so long in vain.
But while I listened for a word
   That should translate them from their pain,
I saw that here and there a face
Shone, and was lifted from its place,

And flashed into the moving dome
   An ecstasy of prismed fire.
And then said I, "A soul has come
   To the deep zenith of desire!"
But still I wondered if it knew
The dream for which it died was true.

I wondered—who shall say how long?
   (One heart-beat?—Thrice ten thousand years?)
Till suddenly there was no throng
   Of faces to arraign the spheres,—
No more white faces there to cry
To those great pageants of the sky.

Then quietly I grew aware
   Of one who came with eyes of bliss
And brow of calm and lips of prayer.
   Said I—"How wonderful is this!
Where are the faces once that cried—
'Give us the dream for which we died'?"

The answer fell as soft as sleep,—
  "I am of those who, having cried
So long in that tumultuous deep,
  Have won the dream for which we died."
And then said I—"Which dream was true?
For many were revealed to you!"

He answered—"To the soul made wise
  All true, all beautiful they seem.
But the white peace that fills our eyes
  Outdoes desire, outreaches dream.
For we are come unto the place
Where always we behold God's face!"

THE FALLING LEAVES

LIGHTLY He blows, and at His breath they fall,
  The perishing kindreds of the leaves; they drift,
Spent flames of scarlet, gold aerial,
  Across the hollow year, noiseless and swift.
Lightly He blows, and countless as the falling
  Of snow by night upon a solemn sea,
The ages circle down beyond recalling,
  To strew the hollows of Eternity.
He sees them drifting through the spaces dim,
  And leaves and ages are as one to Him.

THE SOLITARY WOODSMAN

WHEN the gray lake-water rushes
Past the dripping alder bushes,
  And the bodeful autumn wind
In the fir-tree weeps and hushes,—

When the air is sharply damp
Round the solitary camp,
   And the moose-bush in the thicket
Glimmers like a scarlet lamp,—

When the birches twinkle yellow,
And the cornel bunches mellow,
   And the owl across the twilight
Trumpets to his downy fellow,—

When the nut-fed chipmunks romp
Through the maples' crimson pomp,
   And the slim viburnum flushes
In the darkness of the swamp,—

When the blueberries are dead,
When the rowan clusters red,
   And the shy bear, summer-sleekened,
In the bracken makes his bed,—

On a day there comes once more
To the latched and lonely door,
   Down the wood-road striding silent,
One who has been here before.

Green spruce branches for his head,
Here he makes his simple bed,
   Couching with the sun, and rising
When the dawn is frosty red.

All day long he wanders wide
With the grey moss for his guide,
   And his lonely axe-stroke startles
The expectant forest-side.

Toward the quiet close of day
Back to camp he takes his way,
   And about his sober footsteps
Unafraid the squirrels play.

On his roof the red leaf falls,
At his door the bluejay calls,
   And he hears the wood-mice hurry
Up and down his rough log walls;

Hears the laughter of the loon
Thrill the dying afternoon,—
   Hears the calling of the moose
Echo to the early moon.

And he hears the partridge drumming,
The belated hornet humming,—
   All the faint, prophetic sounds
That foretell the winter's coming.

And the wind about his eaves
Through the chilly night-wet grieves,
   And the earth's dumb patience fills him,
Fellow to the falling leaves.

ICE

WHEN Winter scourged the meadow and the hill
And in the withered leafage worked his will,
The water shrank, and shuddered, and stood still,—
Then built himself a magic house of glass,
Irised with memories of flowers and grass,
Wherein to sit and watch the fury pass.

BOOK OF THE ROSE

1903

THE STRANDED SHIP

FAR UP the lonely strand the storm had lifted her.
And now along her keel the merry tides make stir
No more.   The running waves that sparkled at her prow
Seethe to the chains and sing no more with laughter now.
No more the clean sea-furrow follows her.   No more
To the hum of her gallant tackle the hale Nor'-westers roar.
No more her bulwarks journey.   For the only boon they
    crave
Is the guerdon of all good ships and true, the boon of a
    deep-sea grave.

Take me out, sink me deep in the green profound,
To sway with the long weed, swing with the drowned,
Where the change of the soft tide makes no sound,
Far below the keels of the outward bound.

No more she mounts the circles from Fundy to the Horn,
From Cuba to the Cape runs down the tropic morn,
Explores the Vast Uncharted where great bergs ride in
    ranks,
Nor shouts a broad "Ahoy" to the dories on the Banks.
No more she races freights to Zanzibar and back,
Nor creeps where the fog lies blind along the liners' track,
No more she dares the cyclone's disastrous core of calm
To greet across the dropping wave the amber isles of palm.

Take me out, sink me deep in the green profound,
To sway with the long weed, swing with the drowned,
Where the change of the soft tide makes no sound,
Far below the keels of the outward bound.

Amid her trafficking peers, the wind-wise, journeyed ships,
At the black wharves no more, nor at the weedy slips,
She comes to port with cargo from many a storied clime.
No more to the rough-throat chantey her windlass creaks in
    time.

No more she loads for London with spices from Ceylon,—
With white spruce deals and wheat and apples from St.
    John.
No more from Pernambuco with coffee-bags,—no more
With hides from Buenos Ayres she clears for Baltimore.

    Take me out, sink me deep in the green profound,
    To sway with the long weed, swing with the drowned,
    Where the change of the soft tide makes no sound,
    Far below the keels of the outward bound.

Wan with the slow vicissitudes of wind and rain and sun
How grieves her deck for the sailors whose hearty brawls are
        done!
Only the wandering gull brings word of the open wave,
With shrill scream at her taffrail deriding her alien grave.
Around the keel that raced the dolphin and the shark
Only the sand-wren twitters from barren dawn till dark;
And all the long blank noon the blank sand chafes and mars
The prow once swift to follow the lure of the dancing stars.

    Take me out, sink me deep in the green profound,
    To sway with the long weed, swing with the drowned,
    Where the change of the soft tide makes no sound,
    Far below the keels of the outward bound.

And when the winds are low, and when the tides are still,
And the round moon rises inland over the naked hill,
And o'er her parching seams the dry cloud-shadows pass,
And dry along the land-rim lie the shadows of thin grass,
Then aches her soul with longing to launch and sink away
Where the fine silts lift and settle, the sea-things drift and
        sway,
To make the port of Last Desire, and slumber with her peers
In the tide-wash rocking softly through the unnumbered
        years.

Take me out, sink me deep in the green profound,
To sway with the long weed, swing with the drowned,
Where the change of the soft tide makes no sound,
Far below the keels of the outward bound.

THE FIRST PLOUGHING

CALLS the crow from the pine-tree top
When the April air is still,
He calls to the farmer hitching his team
In the farmyard under the hill.
"Come up," he cries, "come out and come up,
For the high field's ripe to till.
Don't wait for word from the dandelion
Or leave from the daffodil."

Cheeps the flycatcher—"Here old earth
Warms up in the April sun;
And the first ephemera, wings yet wet,
From the mould creep one by one.
Under the fence where the flies frequent
Is the earliest gossamer spun.
Come up from the damp of the valley lands,
For here the winter's done."

Whistles the high-hole out of the grove
His summoning loud and clear:
"Chilly it may be down your way
But the high south field has cheer.
On the sunward side of the chestnut stump
The woodgrubs wake and appear.
Come out to your ploughing, come up to your ploughing,
The time for ploughing is here."

Then drips the coulter and drives the share,
And the furrows faintly steam.
The crow drifts furtively down from the pine
To follow the clanking team.
The flycatcher tumbles, the high-hole darts
In the young noon's yellow gleam;
And wholesome sweet the smell of the sod
Upturned from its winter's dream.

CHILD OF THE INFINITE

SUN, and Moon, and Wind, and Flame,
Dust, and Dew, and Day and Night,—
Ye endure.   Shall I endure not,
Though so fleeting in your sight?
Ye return.   Shall I return not,
Flesh, or in the flesh's respite?
Ye are mighty.   But I hold you
Compassed in a vaster might.

Sun.   Sun, before your flaming circuit
Smote upon the uncumbered dark,
I, within the Thought Eternal
Palpitant, a quenchless spark,
Watched while God awoke and set you
For a measure and a mark.

Moon.   Dove of Heaven, ere you brooded
Whitely o'er the shoreless waste,
And upon the driven waters
Your austere enchantment placed,
I was power in God's conception,
Without rest and without haste.

Wind.   Breath of Time, before your whisper
          Wandered o'er the naked world,
          Ere your wrath from pole to tropic
          Running Alps of ocean hurled,
          I, the germ of storm in stillness,
          At the heart of God lay furled.

Flame.   Journeying Spirit, ere your tongues
          Taught the perished to aspire,
          Charged the clod, and called the mortal
          Through the reinitiant fire,
          I was of the fiery impulse
          Urging the Divine Desire.

Dust.   Seed of Earth, when down the void
          You were scattered from His hand,
          When the spinning clot contracted,
          Globed and greened at His command,
          I, behind the sifting fingers,
          Saw the scheme of beauty planned.

Dew.   Phantom of the Many Waters,
          When no more you fleet and fall,
          When no more your round you follow,
          Infinite, ephemeral,
          At the feet of the Unsleeping
          I shall toss you like a ball.

Day and Rolling Masks of Life and Death,
Night.   When no more your ancient place
          Knows you, when your light and darkness
          Swing no longer over space,
          My remembrance shall restore you
          To the favour of His face.

HEAT IN THE CITY

OVER the scorching roofs of iron
The red moon rises slow.
Uncomforted beneath its light
The pale crowds gasping go.

The heart-sick city, spent with day,
Cries out in vain for sleep.
The childless wife beside her dead
Is too outworn to weep.

The children in the upper rooms
Lie faint, with half-shut eyes.
In the thick-breathing, lighted ward
The stricken workman dies.

From breathless pit and sweltering loft
Dim shapes creep one by one
To throng the curb and crowd the stoops
And fear tomorrow's sun.

WHEN MARY THE MOTHER KISSED THE CHILD

WHEN Mary the Mother kissed the Child
And night on the wintry hills grew mild,
And the strange star swung from the courts of air
To serve at a manger with kings in prayer,
Then did the day of the simple kin
And the unregarded folk begin.

When Mary the Mother forgot the pain,
In the stable of rock began love's reign.
When that new light on their grave eyes broke
The oxen were glad and forgot their yoke;
And the huddled sheep in the far hill fold
Stirred in their sleep and felt no cold.

When Mary the Mother gave of her breast
To the poor inn's latest and lowliest guest,—
The God born out of the woman's side,—
The Babe of Heaven by Earth denied,—
Then did the hurt ones cease to moan,
And the long-supplanted came to their own.

When Mary the Mother felt faint hands
Beat at her bosom with life's demands,
And nought to her were the kneeling kings,
The serving star and the half-seen wings,
Then was the little of earth made great,
And the man came back to the God's estate.

THE GREAT AND THE LITTLE WEAVERS

THE great and the little weavers,
They neither rest nor sleep.
They work in the height and the glory,
They toil in the dark and the deep.

The rainbow melts with the shower,
The white-thorn falls in the gust,
The cloud-rose dies into shadow,
The earth-rose dies into dust.

But they have not faded forever,
They have not flowered in vain,
For the great and the little weavers
Are weaving under the rain.

Recede the drums of the thunder
When the Titan chorus tires,
And the bird-song piercing the sunset
Faints with the sunset fires,

But the trump of the storm shall fail not,
Nor the flute-cry fail of the thrush,
For the great and the little weavers
Are weaving under the hush.

The comet flares into darkness,
The flame dissolves into death,
The power of the star and the dew
They grow and are gone like a breath,

But ere the old wonder is done
Is the new-old wonder begun,
For the great and the little weavers
Are weaving under the sun.

The domes of an empire crumble,
A child's hope dies in tears;
Time rolls them away forgotten
In the silt of the flooding years;

The creed for which men died smiling
Decays to a beldame's curse;
The love that made lips immortal
Drags by in a tattered hearse.

But not till the search of the moon
Sees the last white face uplift,
And over the bones of the kindreds
The bare sands dredge and drift,

Shall Love forget to return
And lift the unused latch,
(In his eyes the look of the traveller,
On his lips the foreign catch),

Nor the mad song leave men cold,
Nor the high dream summon in vain,—
For the great and the little weavers
Are weaving in heart and brain.

THE AIM

O THOU who lovest not alone
The swift success, the instant goal,
But hast a lenient eye to mark
The failures of the inconstant soul,

Consider not my little worth,—
The mean achievement, scamped in act,
The high resolve and low result,
The dream that durst not face the fact.

But count the reach of my desire.
Let this be something in Thy sight;—
I have not, in the slothful dark,
Forgot the Vision and the Height.

Neither my body nor my soul
To earth's low ease will yield consent.
I praise Thee for my will to strive.
I bless Thy goad of discontent.

NEW POEMS

1919

MONITION

A FAINT wind, blowing from World's End,
  Made strange the city street.
A strange sound mingled in the fall
  Of the familiar feet.

Something unseen whirled with the leaves
  To tap on door and sill.
Something unknown went whispering by
  Even when the wind was still.

And men looked up with startled eyes
  And hurried on their way,
As if they had been called, and told
  How brief their day.

HILL TOP SONG

WHEN the lights come out in the cottages
  Along the shores at eve,
And across the darkening water
  The last pale shadows leave;

And up from the rock-ridged pasture slopes
  The sheep-bell tinklings steal,
And the folds are shut, and the shepherds
  Turn to their quiet meal;

And even here, on the unfenced height,
  No journeying wind goes by,
But the earth-sweet smells, and the home-sweet sounds,
  Mount, like prayer, to the sky;

Then from the door of my opened heart
  Old blindness and pride are driven,
Till I know how high is the humble,
  The dear earth how close to heaven.

UNDER THE PILLARS OF THE SKY

UNDER the pillars of the sky
I played at life, I knew not why.

The grave recurrence of the day
Was matter of my trivial play.

The solemn stars, the sacred night,
I took for toys of my delight,

Till now, with startled eyes, I see
The portents of Eternity.

EASTWARD BOUND

WE MOUNT the arc of ocean's round
  To meet the splendours of the sun;
Then downward rush into the dark
  When the blue, spacious day is done.

The slow, eternal drift of stars
  Draws over us until the dawn.
Then the grey steep we mount once more,
  And the night is down the void withdrawn.

Space, and interminable hours,
  And moons that rise, and sweep, and fall,—
On-swinging earth, and orbéd sea,—
  And voyaging souls more vast than all!

THE PLACE OF HIS REST

THE green marsh-mallows
  Are over him.
Along the shallows
  The pale lights swim.

Wide air, washed grasses,
  And waveless stream;
And over him passes
  The drift of dream;—

The pearl-hue down
  Of the poplar seed;
The elm-flower brown;
  And the sway of the reed;

The blue moth, winged
  With a flake of sky;
The bee, gold ringed;
  And the dragon-fly.

Lightly the rushes,
  Lean to his breast;
A bird's wing brushes
  The place of his rest.

The far-flown swallow,
  The gold-finch flame,—
They come, they follow
  The paths he came.

    .   .   .

And while around him
  The kind grass creeps,
Where peace hath found him
  How sound he sleeps.

Well to his slumber
    Attends the year:
Soft rains without number
    Soft noons, blue clear,

With nights of balm,
    And the dark, sweet hours
Brooding with calm,
    Pregnant with flowers.

See how she speeds them,
    Each childlike bloom,
And softly leads them
    To tend his tomb!

THE SUMMONS

DEEPS of the wind-torn west,
    Flaming and desolate,
Upsprings my soul from his rest
    With your banners at the gate.

'Neath this o'ermastering sky
    How could the heart lie still,
    Or the sluggish will
Content in the old chains lie,
    When over the lonely hill
Your torn wild scarlets cry?

Up, Soul, and out
    Into the deeps alone,
To the long peal and the shout
    Of those trumpets blown and blown!

THE VAGRANT OF TIME
1927

THE VAGRANT OF TIME

I VOYAGE north, I journey south,
  I taste the life of many lands,
With ready wonder in my eyes
  And strong adventure in my hands.

I join the young-eyed caravans
  That storm the portals of the West;
And sometimes in their throng I catch
  Hints of the secret of my quest.

The musks and attars of the East,
  Expecting marvels, I explore.
I chase them down the dim bazaar,
  I guess them through the close-shut door.

In the lone cabin, sheathed in snow,
  I bide a season, well content,
Till forth again I needs must fare,
  Called by an unknown continent.

I loiter down remembered shores
  Where restless tide-flows lift and surge,—
In my wild heart their restlessness
  And in my veins their tireless urge.

In old grey cities oft I dwell,
  Down storied rivers drift and dream.
Sometimes in palaces I lose,
  Sometimes in hovels catch, the gleam.

Great fortune in my wayfaring
  I stumble on, more oft than not,—
Grip comrade hands in hall or camp,
  Greet ardent lips in court or cot.

Down country lanes at noon I stray,
  Loaf in the homely wayside heat,
And with bright flies and droning bees
  Rifle the buckwheat of its sweet.

In solitudes of peak or plain,
  When vaulted space my sense unbars,
I pitch my tent, and camp the night
  Beyond the unfathomed gulfs of stars.

At times I thirst, at times I faint,
  Sink mired in swamp, stray blind in storm,
See high hopes shattered, faiths betrayed,—
  But stout heart keeps my courage warm.

And sometimes rock-ridged steeps I climb
  In chill black hours before the dawn.
With battered shins and bleeding feet
  And obstinate fists I blunder on.

And then, when sunrise floods my path,
  I pause to build my dreams anew.
But, take the gipsying all in all,
  I find a-many dreams come true.

So when, one night, I drop my pack
  Behind the Last Inn's shadowy door,
To take my rest in that lone room
  Where no guest ever lodged before,

In sleep too deep for dreams I'll lie,—
  Till One shall knock, and bid me rise
To quest new ventures, fare new roads,
  Essay new suns and vaster skies.

IN THE NIGHT WATCHES

WHEN the little spent winds are at rest in the tamarack
      tree
In the still of the night,
And the moon in her waning is wan and misshapen,
And out on the lake
The loon floats in a glimmer of light,
And the solitude sleeps,—
Then I lie in my bunk wide awake,
And my long thoughts stab me with longing,
Alone in my shack by the marshes of lone Margaree.

Far, oh so far in the forests of silence they lie,
The lake and the marshes of lone Margaree,
And no man comes my way.
Of spruce logs my cabin is builded securely;
With slender spruce saplings its bark roof is battened down
      surely;
In its rafters the mice are at play,
With rustlings furtive and shy,
In the still of the night.

Awake, wide-eyed I watch my window-square,
Pallid and grey.
(O Memory, pierce me not!   O Longing, stab me not!
O ache of longing memory, pass me by, and spare,
And let me sleep!)
Once and again the loon cries from the lake.
Though no breath stirs
The ghostly tamaracks and the brooding firs,
Something as light as air leans on my door.

Is it an owl's wing brushes at my latch?
Are they of foxes, those light feet that creep
Outside, light as fall'n leaves
On the forest floor?

From the still lake I hear
A feeding trout rise to some small night fly.
The splash, how sharply clear!
Almost I see the wide, slow ripple circling to the shore.

The spent winds are at rest.   But my heart, spent and faint,
      is unresting,
Long, long a stranger to peace . . .
O so Dear, O so Far, O so Unforgotten-in-dream,
Somewhere in the world, somewhere beyond reach of my
      questing.
Beyond seas, beyond years,
You will hear my heart in your sleep, and you will stir
      restlessly;
You will stir at the touch of my hand on your hair;
You will wake with a start,
With my voice in your ears
And an old, old ache at your heart,
(In the still of the night)
And your pillow wet with tears.

HATH HOPE KEPT VIGIL

FRAIL lilies that beneath the dust so long
    Have lain in cerements of musk and slumber,
While over you hath fled the viewless throng
    Of hours and winds and voices out of number,

Pulseless and dead in that enswathing dark
    Hath hope kept vigil at your core of being?
Did the germ know what unextinguished spark
    Held these white blooms within its heart unseeing?

Once more into the dark when I go down,
    And deep and deaf the black clay seals my prison,
Will the numbed soul foreknow how light shall crown
    With strong young ecstasy its life new risen?

SPRING BREAKS IN FOAM

SPRING breaks in foam
   Along the blackthorn bough.
Whitethroat and goldenwing
   Are mating now.
With green buds in the copse
   And gold bloom in the sun
Earth is one ecstasy
   Of life begun.
And in my heart
   Spring breaks in glad surprise
As the long frosts of the long years melt
   At your dear eyes.

TODAY

AS ONCE by Hybna's emerald flow
   The goatboy saw in dream
The old gods to their hunting go,
   And heard their eagles scream,
So I, by Nashwaak's amber stream,
   See gods and heroes pass,
While these drab days and deeds but seem
   Like shadows in a glass.

But when a thousand years are done
   My eyes, unsealed, will know
Beauty and glory new begun
   As in the long ago;
And then, astonished, I shall know
   The splendour of Today,
When men outdare the old gods, and grow
   In reach more vast than they.

PHILANDER'S SONG

I SAT and read Anacreon.
  Moved by the gay, delicious measure
I mused that lips were made for love,
  And love to charm a poet's leisure.

And as I mused a maid came by
  With something in her look that caught me.
Forgotten was Anacreon's line,
  But not the lesson he had taught me.

THE ICEBERG AND
OTHER POEMS

1934

THE ICEBERG

I WAS spawned from the glacier,
A thousand miles due north
Beyond Cape Chidley;
And the spawning,
When my vast, wallowing bulk went under,
Emerged and heaved aloft,
Shaking down cataracts from its rocking sides,
With mountainous surge and thunder
Outraged the silence of the Arctic sea.

Before I was thrust forth
A thousand years I crept,
Crawling, crawling, crawling irresistibly,
Hid in the blue womb of the eternal ice,
While under me the tortured rock
Groaned,
And over me the immeasurable desolation slept.

Under the pallid dawning
Of the lidless Arctic day
Forever no life stirred.
No wing of bird—
Of ghostly owl low winnowing
Or fleet-winged ptarmigan fleeing the pounce of death,—
No foot of backward-glancing fox
Half glimpsed and vanishing like a breath,—
No lean and gauntly stalking bear,
Stalking his prey.
Only the white sun, circling the white sky.
Only the wind screaming perpetually.

And then the night—
The long night, naked, high over the roof of the world,
Where time seemed frozen in the cold of space,—
Now black, and torn with cry
Of unseen voices where the storm raged by,
Now radiant with spectral light
As the vault of heaven split wide
To let the flaming Polar cohorts through,
And close ranked spears of gold and blue,
Thin scarlet and thin green,
Hurtled and clashed across the sphere
And hissed in sibilant whisperings,
And died.
And then the stark moon, swinging low,
Silver, indifferent, serene,
Over the sheeted snow.

But now, an Alp afloat,
In seizure of the surreptitious tide,
Began my long drift south to a remote
And unimagined doom.
Scornful of storm,
Unjarred by thunderous buffeting of seas,
Shearing the giant floes aside,
Ploughing the wide-flung ice-fields in a spume
That smoked far up my ponderous flanks,
Onward I fared,
My ice-blue pinnacles rendering back the sun
In darts of sharp radiance;
My bases fathoms deep in the dark profound.

And now around me
Life, and the frigid waters all aswarm.
The smooth wave creamed
With tiny capelin and the small pale squid,—
So pale the light struck through them.

Gulls and gannets screamed
Over the feast, and gorged themselves, and rose,
A clamour of weaving wings, and hid
Momently my face.
The great bull whales
With cavernous jaws agape,
Scooped in the spoil, and slept,
Their humped forms just awash, and rocking softly,—
Or sounded down, down to the deeps, and nosed
Along my ribbed and sunken roots,
And in the green gloom scattered the pasturing cod.

   And so I voyaged on, down the dim parallels,
Convoyed by fields
Of countless calving seals
Mild-featured, innocent-eyed, and unforeknowing
The doom of the red flenching knives.
I passed the storm-racked gate
Of Hudson Strait,
And savage Chidley where the warring tides
In white wrath seethe forever.
Down along the sounding shore
Of iron-fanged, many-watered Labrador
Slow weeks I shaped my course, and saw
Dark Mokkowic and dark Napiskawa,
And came at last off lone Belle Isle, the bane
Of ships and snare of bergs.
Here, by the deep conflicting currents drawn,
I hung,
And swung,
The inland voices Gulfward calling me
To ground amid my peers on the alien strand
And roam no more.
But then an off-shore wind,
A great wind fraught with fate,
Caught me and pressed me back,
And I resumed my solitary way.

Slowly I bore
South-east by bastioned Bauld,
And passed the sentinel light far-beaming late
Along the liners' track,
And slanted out Atlanticwards, until
Above the treacherous swaths of fog
Faded from view the loom of Newfoundland.

  Beautiful, ethereal
In the blue sparkle of the gleaming day,
A soaring miracle
Of white immensity,
I was the cynosure of passing ships
That wondered and were gone,
Their wreathed smoke trailing them beyond the verge.
And when in the night they passed—
The night of stars and calms,
Forged up and passed, with churning surge
And throb of huge propellers, and long-drawn
Luminous wake behind,
And sharp, small lights in rows,
I lay a ghost of menace chill and still,
A shape pearl-pale and monstrous, off to leeward,
Blurring the dim horizon line.

  Day dragged on day,
And then came fog,
By noon, blind-white,
And in the night
Black-thick and smothering the sight.
Folded therein I waited,
Waited I knew not what
And heeded not,
Greatly incurious and unconcerned,
I heard the small waves lapping along my base,
Lipping and whispering, lisping with bated breath
A casual expectancy of death.

I heard remote
The deep, far carrying note
Blown from the hoarse and hollow throat
Of some lone tanker groping on her course.
Louder and louder rose the sound
In deepening diapason, then passed on,
Diminishing, and dying,—
And silence closed around.
And in the silence came again
Those stealthy voices,
That whispering of death.

    And then I heard
The thud of screws approaching.
Near and more near,
Louder and yet more loud,
Through the thick dark I heard it,—
The rush and hiss of waters as she ploughed
Head on, unseen, unseeing,
Toward where I stood across her path, invisible.
And then a startled blare
Of horror close re-echoing,—a glare
Of sudden, stabbing searchlights
That but obscurely pierced the gloom;
And there
I towered, a dim immensity of doom.

    A roar
Of tortured waters as the giant screws,
Reversed, thundered full steam astern.
Yet forward still she drew, until,
Slow answering desperate helm,
She swerved, and all her broadside came in view,
Crawling beneath me;

And for a moment I saw faces, blanched,
Stiffly agape, turned upward, and wild eyes
Astare; and one long, quavering cry went up
As a submerged horn gored her through and through,
Ripping her beam wide open;
And sullenly she listed, till her funnels
Crashed on my steep,
And men sprang, stumbling, for the boats.

But now, my deep foundations
Mined by those warmer seas, the hour had come
When I must change.
Slowly I leaned above her,
Slowly at first, then faster,
And icy fragments rained upon her decks.
Then my enormous mass descended on her,
A falling mountain, all obliterating,—
And the confusion of thin, wailing cries,
The Babel of shouts and prayers
And shriek of steam escaping
Suddenly died.
And I rolled over,
Wallowing,
And once more came to rest,
My long hid bases heaved up high in air.

    And now, from fogs emerging,
I traversed blander seas,
Forgot the fogs, the scourging
Of sleet-whipped gales, forgot
My austere origin, my tremendous birth,
My journeyings, and that last cataclysm
Of overwhelming ruin.
My squat, pale, alien bulk
Basked in the ambient sheen;
And all about me, league on league outspread,
A gulf of indigo and green.

I laughed in the light waves laced with white,—
Nor knew
How swiftly shrank my girth
Under their sly caresses, how the breath
Of that soft wind sucked up my strength, nor how
The sweet, insidious fingers of the sun
Their stealthy depredations wrought upon me.

   Slowly now
I drifted, dreaming.
I saw the flying-fish
With silver gleaming
Flash from the peacock-bosomed wave
And flicker through an arc of sunlit air
Back to their element, desperate to elude
The jaws of the pursuing albacore.

   Day after day
I swung in the unhasting tide.
Sometimes I saw the dolphin folk at play,
Their lithe sides iridescent-dyed,
Unheeding in their speed
That long grey wraith,
The shark that followed hungering beneath.
Sometimes I saw a school
Of porpoise rolling by
In ranked array,
Emerging and submerging rhythmically,
Their blunt black bodies heading all one way
Until they faded
In the horizon's dazzling line of light.
Night after night
I followed the low, large moon across the sky,
Or counted the large stars on the purple dark,
The while I wasted, wasted and took no thought,
In drowsed entrancement caught;—

Until one noon a wave washed over me,
Breathed low a sobbing sigh,
Foamed indolently, and passed on;
And then I knew my empery was gone;
As I, too, soon must go.
And well content I was to have it so.

    Another night
Gloomed o'er my sight,
With cloud, and flurries of warm, wild rain.
Another day,
Dawning delectably
With amber and scarlet stain,
Swept on its way,
Glowing and shimmering with heavy heat.
A lazing tuna rose
And nosed me curiously,
And shouldered me aside in brusque disdain,
So had I fallen from my high estate.
A foraging gull
Stooped over me, touched me with webbed pink feet,
And wheeled and skreeled away,
Indignant at the chill.

    Last I became
A little glancing globe of cold
That slid and sparkled on the slow-pulsed swell.
And then my fragile, scintillating frame
Dissolved in ecstasy
Of many coloured light,
And I breathed up my soul into the air
And merged forever in the all-solvent sea.

TAORMINA

A LITTLE tumbled city on the height,
  Basking above the cactus and the sea!
What pale, frail ghosts of memory come tonight
  And call back the forgotten years to me!
    Taormina, Taormina,
    And the month of the almond blossom.

In an old book I find a withered flower,
  And withered dreams awake to their old fire.
How far have danced your feet since that fair hour
  That brought us to the land of heart's desire!
    Taormina, Taormina,
    Oh, the scent of the almond blossom.

The grey-white monastery-garden wall
  O'erpeers the white crag, and the flung vines upclamber
In the white sun, and cling and seem to fall,—
  Brave bougainvilleas, purple and smoky amber.
    Taormina, Taormina,
    And the month of the almond blossom.

You caught your breath, as hand in hand we stood
  To watch the luminous peak of Aetna there
Soaring above the cloudy solitude,
  Enmeshed in the opaline Sicilian air.
    Taormina, Taormina,
    Oh, the scent of the almond blossom.

We babbled of Battos and brown Corydon,—
  Of Amaryllis coiling her dark locks,—
Of the sad-hearted satyr grieving on
  The tomb of Helicè among the rocks
  O'erhung with the almond blossom,—

Of how the goat-boy wrenched apart the vines
   That veiled the slim-limbed Chloe at her bath,
And followed her fleet-foot flight among the pines
   And caught her close, and kissed away her wrath.
      Taormina, Taormina,
      And the month of the almond blossom.

And then—you turned impetuously to me!
   We saw the blue hyacinths at our feet; and came
To the battlements, and looked down upon the sea—
   And the sea was a blue flame!

                 .   .   .

The blue flame dies.   The ghosts come back to me.
      Taormina, Taormina,
      Oh, the scent of the almond blossom.

BE QUIET, WIND

BE QUIET, wind, a little while,
   And let me hear my heart.
You chiming rivulet, still your chant
   And stealthily depart.

You whisperings in the aspen leaves,
   You far-heard whip-poor-will,
You slow drop spilling from the rose—
   You, even you, be still.

I must have infinite silence now,
   Lest I should miss one word
Of all my heart would say to me—
   Now, when its deeps are stirred.

Hardly I dare my breath to draw
   Lest breathing break the spell,—
While we commune, my heart and I,
   In dreams too deep to tell.

THE SQUATTER

ROUND the lone clearing
Clearly the whitethroats call
Across the marge of dusk and the dewfall's coolness.

Far up in the empty
Amber and apple-green sky
A night-hawk swoops and twangs her silver chord.

No wind's astir,
But the poplar boughs breathe softly
And the smoke of a dying brush-fire stings the air.

The spired, dark spruces
Crowd up to the snake fence, breathless,
Expectant till the rising of the moon.

In the wet alders,
Where the cold brook flows murmuring,
The red cow drinks,—the cow-bell sounds *tonk-tonk*.

.   .   .

From his cabin door
The squatter lounges forth,
Sniffs the damp air, and scans the sky for rain.

He has made his meal,—
Fat bacon, and buckwheat cakes,
And ruddy-brown molasses from Barbados.

His chores all done,
He seats himself on the door-sill,
And slowly fills his pipe, and smokes, and dreams.

He sees his axe
Leaning against the birch logs.
The fresh white chips are scattered over the yard.

He hears his old horse
Nosing the hay, in the log barn
Roofed with poles and sheathed with sheets of birch-bark.

Beyond the barn
He sees his buckwheat patch,
Its pink-white bloom pale-gleaming through the twilight.

Its honeyed fragrance
Breathes to his nostrils, mingled
With the tang of the brush-fire smoke, thinly ascending.

Deepens the dusk.
The whitethroats are hushed; and the night-hawk
Drops down from the sky and hunts the low-flying night-
    moths.   .   .   .

The squatter is dreaming.
Vaguely he plans how, come winter,
He'll chop out another field, just over the brook.

He'll build a new barn
Next year, a barn with a haymow,
No more to leave his good hay outside in the stack.

He rises and stretches,
Goes in and closes the door,
And lights his lamp on the table beside the window.

The light shines forth.
It lights up the wide-strewn chips.
For a moment it catches the dog darting after a rabbit.

It lights up the lean face
Of the squatter as he sits reading,
Knitting his brow as he spells out a month-old paper.

. . .

Slowly the moon,
Humped, crooked, red, remote,
Rises, tangled and scrawled behind the spruce-tops.

Higher she rises,—
Grows rounder, and smaller, and white,
And sails up the empty sky high over the spruce-tops.

She washes in silver,
Illusively clear, the log barn,
The lop-sided stack by the barn, and the slumbering cabin.

She floods in the window,—.
And the squatter stirs in his bunk,
On his mattress stuffed with green fir-tips, balsamy scented.

. . .

From the dark of the forest
The horned owl hoots, and is still.
Startled, the silence descends, and broods once more on the
    clearing.

WESTCOCK HILL

AS I came over Westcock Hill
  My heart was full of tears.
Under the summer's pomp I heard
  The spending of the years.
Oh, the sweet years!   The swift years!
  The years that lapse away!

I saw the green slopes bathed in sun.
　The marshlands stretched afar,
And, hurrying pale between its dikes.
　My memoried Tantramar.
Oh, the sweet years!   The swift years!
　The years that lapse away!

The salt tang and the buckwheat scents
　Were on the breathing air;
And all was glad.   But I was sad
　For one who was not there.
Oh, the sweet years!   The swift years!
　The years that lapse away!

I wandered down to Westcock Church,
　The old grey church in the wood.
Kneeling, I heard my father's voice
　In that hushed solitude.
Oh, the sweet years!   The swift years!
　The years that lapse away!

I saw again his surpliced form.
　I heard the hymning choir.
Shadows!—and dreams!   Alone remained
　The ache of my desire.
Oh, the sweet years!   The swift years!
The years that lapse away!

He sleeps;—how many a year removed,
　How many a league withdrawn
From these dear woods, these turbid floods,
　These fields that front the dawn.
Oh, the sweet years!   The swift years!
　The years have lapsed away!

BIBLIOGRAPHICAL NOTE

Roberts' own chief books of verse are listed chronologically, with their dates, in the Table of Contents. The only full-length biography of Roberts is that by Elsie M. Pomeroy, *Sir Charles G. D. Roberts: A Biography,* published by The Ryerson Press, Toronto, in 1943. A more informal approach to his life and personality will be found in *The Book of Roberts* written by his son, Lloyd Roberts, and published by The Ryerson Press in 1924. There are two books of criticism, both written by James Cappon: *Roberts and the Influences of His Time* (Toronto, 1905) and *Charles G. D. Roberts* (Toronto, 1925). Briefer critical treatment may be found in all of the histories and handbooks of Canadian literature, and notably in E. K. Brown's *On Canadian Poetry* (Toronto, 1943); Archibald MacMechan's *Headwaters of Canadian Literature* (Toronto, 1924); my own *Creative Writing in Canada* (Toronto, 1952); W. P. Percival's *Leading Canadian Poets* (Toronto, 1948); Lorne Pierce's *Outline of Canadian Literature* (Toronto, 1927); and V. B. Rhodenizer's *Handbook of Canadian Literature* (Ottawa, 1930).

The following magazine articles will also be found useful:

Pelham Edgar: "Sir Charles G. D. Roberts and His Times", *University of Toronto Quarterly,* 13: 117-126 (October, 1943).

Archibald Lampman: "Two Canadian Poets", *University of Toronto Quarterly,* 13: 406-423 (July, 1944).

T. G. Marquis: "Professor Charles G. D. Roberts, M.A.", *The Week,* V: 558-9 (July 26, 1888).

T. G. Marquis: "Roberts", *Canadian Magazine* I: 572-5 (September, 1893).

T. G. Marquis: "Songs of the Common Day", *The Week,*
    X: 1023 (September 22, 1893).   (The most perceptive
    contemporary review of Roberts' best book of verse.)

B. Muddiman: "A Vignette in Canadian Literature", *Canadian
    Magazine,* XL: 451-8 (March, 1913).

A. M. Stephen: "The Poetry of Charles G. D. Roberts",
    Queen's Quarterly, XXXVI: 48-64 (January, 1929).